SOUTH DOWNS WALK

Warne Gerrard Guides for Walkers

SOUTH DOWNS

WALKS FOR MOTORISTS

Ben Perkins

Sketch maps by Chartwell Illustrators
6 photographs by Denis Perkins

FREDERICK WARNE

Published by
Frederick Warne (Publishers) Ltd
40 Bedford Square,
London WC1B 3HE

© Frederick Warne (Publishers) Ltd

First published 1979
Reprinted (with revisions) 1980

The picture on the front cover shows a path near Fulking and that on the back cover shows the approach to Mount Caburn. Both photographs were taken by Denis Perkins, as were those inside the book.

Publishers' Note
While every care has been taken in the compilation of this book, the publishers cannot accept responsibility for any inaccuracies. Things may have changed since the book was published: paths are sometimes diverted, a concrete bridge may replace a wooden one, stiles disappear. Please let the publishers know if you discover anything like this on your way.

The length of each walk in this book is given in miles and kilometres, but within the text Imperial measurements are quoted. It is useful to bear the following approximations in mind: 5 miles = 8 kilometres, $\frac{1}{2}$ mile = 805 metres, 1 metre = 39.4 inches.

ISBN 0 7232 2146 4

Phototypeset by Tradespools Limited, Frome, Somerset
Printed by Galava Printing Co. Ltd., Nelson, Lancashire
1445.580

Contents

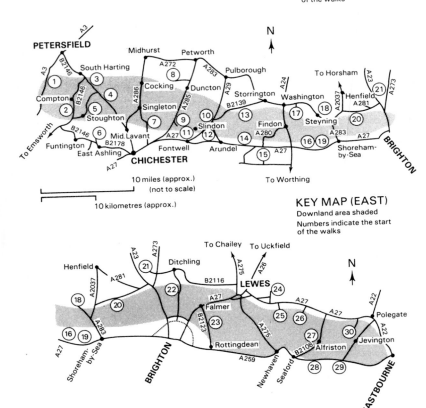

KEY MAP (WEST)
Downland area shaded
Numbers indicate the start
of the walks

N

PETERSFIELD
Midhurst   Petworth
South Harting
A272
Cocking   Duncton   Pulborough   To Horsham
Compton   Singleton   Storrington   Washington   Henfield
Stoughton   Slindon   Findon   Steyning
Mid.Lavant   Funtington
East Ashling   Fontwell   Arundel   Shoreham-by-Sea
CHICHESTER
To Emsworth
To Worthing   BRIGHTON

10 miles (approx.)
(not to scale)

10 kilometres (approx.)

KEY MAP (EAST)
Downland area shaded
Numbers indicate the start
of the walks

To Chailey   To Uckfield
Henfield   Ditchling
LEWES
B2116
Falmer
Shoreham-by-Sea   Rottingdean   Alfriston   Polegate
BRIGHTON   Newhaven   Seaford   Jevington
EASTBOURNE

N

Introduction

The thirty walks in this book are spread out over the entire length of the South Downs in East and West Sussex, from Butser Hill just over the Hampshire border (Walk 1) to the hills above Eastbourne (Walk 30). They are fairly evenly distributed though there may be a slight bias in favour of the more extensively wooded downland in West Sussex.

As a rough guide, the following centres might provide a suitable base for the walks indicated.

Chichester	Walks 1–8
Arundel	Walks 9–14
Worthing	Walks 15–18
Brighton	Walks 19–23
Lewes	Walks 24–26
Seaford or Eastbourne	Walks 27–30

The individual walks vary in length between $3\frac{1}{2}$ and 9 miles. They are all circular, starting and finishing at points where there should normally be ample parking space available. For leisurely walking, allow 2 miles an hour plus time for stops. I have not specifically mentioned refreshment facilities in the descriptions, but pubs on the routes are marked on the sketch maps.

For more energetic ramblers who might prefer a longer walk, I have designed a number of the circuits so that they can be linked together in pairs, using one starting point. The link points and routes are indicated in the text and on the sketch maps.

Walk 4 may be linked with Walks 5 and/or 6 to give a total distance of $9\frac{1}{2}$, 11 or $16\frac{1}{2}$ miles.

Walks 9 and 10 combine to give a fairly strenuous 18-mile circuit.

Walks 11 and 12 may be linked to give a total of 11 miles.

Walks 14 and 15 together make $13\frac{1}{2}$ miles.

Walks 16 and 19 combine to give $12\frac{1}{2}$ miles.

Walks 25 and 26 together give a 13-mile trek.

Walks 27 and 30 together make $14\frac{1}{2}$ miles including a 2-mile link route.

Walks 28 and 29 provide $11\frac{1}{2}$ miles through the 'Heritage Coast' area.

Although it should be possible to complete the walks using only the route descriptions and the sketch maps, I certainly would not recommend attempting them without an Ordnance Survey map. The sketch maps are not to scale and provide, in any case, a guide only to features actually on the route of the walk. For rambling in the relatively uncluttered downland landscape the 1:50,000 scale OS maps are generally quite adequate and the latest editions indicate rights of way in red. To cover all the walks in the book you will need three sheets, Numbers 197, 198 and 199, and before each walk I have indicated which particular map will be required. An OS map will enable you to find your way to the starting points of the walks, for which I have included a grid reference in each case. It will also allow you to put the walk in the context of the surrounding countryside and to pick out more distant features not shown on the sketch map. It might also be most valuable if you do happen, in error, to wander off the described route or choose to modify or extend a particular walk.

The Country Code
Guard against all risk of fire.
Fasten all gates.
Keep dogs under proper control.
Keep to the paths across farm land.
Avoid damaging fences, hedges and walls.
Leave no litter.
Safeguard water supplies.
Protect wild life, wild plants and trees.
Go carefully on country roads.
Respect the life of the countryside.

A word about signposting and maintenance of paths. In West Sussex you will find that many of the paths have been waymarked with wooden signposts. These are easily vandalized, however, and have a habit of disappearing. I have, therefore, deliberately omitted almost all reference to them in the written walk descriptions. For the last eight years, West Sussex County Council has been carrying out an extensive review of all rights of way in the county. Although the review has threatened to extinguish a number of good paths (one or two under the axe are included in the walks in this book, but alternative paths, should the closures go through, are indicated in the text), it has also produced a few (though not enough) completely new rights of way and I have included several of these: the splendid paths over Perry Hill (Walk 13) and Steep Down (Walk 19) are two good examples.

East Sussex, in contrast, spends very little money on rights of way. Only in the Heritage Coast area (Walks 28 and 29) has any large-scale waymarking been attempted. Luckily, however, in the downland area most of the paths are well established and regularly walked so there are few problems and, at the time of writing, there are no serious obstructions on the walks included in this book.

All the walks follow public rights of way or paths where public access is permitted or recognized (often on National Trust land). Occasionally, where a path has been obstructed on its true line I have had to deviate a little but whenever this has been necessary I have indicated it in the route description.

If you enjoy the walks in this book and would like to help combat the frequent threats of encroachment on to the Downs by trunk road and urban development, you might consider joining the Society of Sussex Downsmen. Founded in 1923, the Society's main objects are the conservation of the South Downs and the encouragement of their use for quiet recreation. More information about the Society's work and membership application forms may be obtained from the Secretary at 93 Church Road, Hove BN3 2BA, East Sussex.

If you live in Sussex and would like to help with the maintenance and improvement of the paths, the Sussex Rights of Way Group organizes a regular programme of weekend path clearances throughout the year and we would always welcome additional volunteers.

In the preparation of this book, I am glad to acknowledge the help of my father, Denis Perkins. He has provided much of the background information included with the walks and has taken all the photographs. It was he who introduced me to the pleasures of downland walking at an early age, and I am delighted that he has agreed to write the introductory article on the South Downs which follows.

Ben Perkins

The South Downs

The South Downs stretch for eighty miles, from Beachy Head, where they rise up out of the sea, to Butser Hill in Hampshire, which is over twelve miles inland. These 'blunt, bowheaded, whalebacked Downs', as Kipling called them, are visible from almost everywhere in Sussex. They are your southern horizon whenever you see them from the Weald – a gently undulating skyline, ragged with woodland in the western half of the county, smooth and clean-cut in the eastern half, where the sea lies hidden only a few miles beyond. They are a modest range of hills, only 813 feet high at Ditchling Beacon and 836 at Tegleaze Hill, the highest points in East and West Sussex, but strangely impressive as you approach their steep northern escarpment, almost cliff-like in places. It is fascinating to see how the hill-shapes and their relationship to one another change as you cross the Weald, outlying headlands like Wolstonbury and Mount Caburn alternately merging with the rest of the Downs or standing clearly detached.

These Downs are solid chalk, a limestone which is the result of billions of minute sea-shells living and dying beneath ancient seas. Both North and South Downs are the remains of an immense submarine dome of chalk which once covered the Weald to the height of possibly two or three thousand feet, with Ashdown Forest an island in the middle of the sea. To the layman, this is one of geology's more comprehensible theories. The Downs really do look as though this might have happened, and it is not too difficult to imagine how millions of years of erosion have left the gaps through the hills which now connect Weald with coastal plain and sea. There are not many of them; four river valleys, carrying the Arun, Adur, Ouse and Cuckmere, and four dry valleys with main roads. A few other roads cross the Downs by climbing the escarpment diagonally in the manner of ancient trackways, which once perhaps they were. It is not much in eighty miles and partly explains why the Downs seem lonely and empty in spite of the proximity of the crowded coastal plain.

It is the chalk which gives the Downs their special character. Chalk is porous like a sponge and quickly absorbs the rainfall, which then breaks out in springs where the chalk meets sandstone or clay lower down. This can be seen at Fulking (Walk 20), where the water gushes out by the roadside, or at West Firle (Walk 25), where there is an old spring in the middle of the village. These are two of the spring-line villages strung out along the foot of the northern escarpment, often only a mile or so apart. There are also villages in the valleys, especially the river valleys, but very few on the hill-tops.

It is also partly the chalk which determines what will grow in the thin skin of soil which covers it. This soil is poor, dry and wind-swept and for centuries has been mostly grassland, mixed with an amazing variety of small low-growing plants, including cowslips in spring and the wild thyme which used to give the Downs their special summer smell. In autumn festoons of Old Man's Beard whiten patches of scrub or woodland. White is a characteristic feature of the downland landscape; white ploughed fields, old chalk pits, worn tracks climbing hillsides, chalk cliffs. And the flowers determine the birds and butterflies. There is an exquisite butterfly called the Chalkhill Blue. To the ordinary walker the most notable birds of the downland are the joyously-singing larks rising everywhere from grass or cornfield and the birds hovering in the updraught from the escarpment, especially when the wind is in the north, the seagulls, lapwings and occasional kestrels.

Until modern times, it was the chalk which determined the choice of building material in downland villages. Flints are plentiful in chalk. Brick, stone and timber being hard to come by, flint was used for church and cottage alike. The same grey flints thickly litter the arable fields surrounding the groups of flint buildings, which look a natural part of the landscape.

The Cuckmere is the only undeveloped river mouth in Sussex, but none of the rivers is very large and the downland stretch of the Arun is even more beautiful than the Cuckmere valley. These are the West Sussex Downs and thickly wooded. Near Arundel the beech hangers of Arundel Park fall almost vertically to the riverbank. There seems to be no simple explanation of why the Downs west of the Arun should be so different. There are isolated clumps of beech everywhere on the Downs, but to the west there are whole forests, both young and mature, as well as mixed woodland and more yews than anywhere else in the British Isles. The hills are not so steep but the woods are glorious all through the year and there is always a good chance of seeing a few fallow deer running across a forest ride.

It is thought that left alone the Downs everywhere would revert to woodland, but man has prevented this. The primitive agriculture of Neolithic man followed by the nibbling sheep of the medieval wool industry left the Downs looking as I can remember them when I was a boy – miles and miles of bare, sweet-smelling, short-cropped turf. It is probably significant that *dun* in Old English meant a hill, but by the Middle Ages a *doun* meant a sheepwalk; and that the eastern end of the Downs was always more associated with sheep than the west. This might explain why there are more trees west of the Arun.

The sheep have almost disappeared and except on the steep slopes the downland turf has been replaced by vast arable fields. This is the result of economics, aided by modern farm machinery. Widespread ploughing began during the Second World War. It is a big change; and yet it is strange to look through a schoolboy collection of snapshots taken on the South Downs between Eastbourne and Seaford, dated August 1922, and see how much is unchanged. There

11

was little traffic and the roads were rough and narrow and thick with crushed flint. The bus warned you of its approach by appearing in the distance as a tiny white cloud of dust. Friston Mill has gone and so has the team of black oxen ploughing on the hill above Exceat Farm. But the 'little, lost, Down churches' look much the same, and the ox-bow curves of the Cuckmere river, and the shape of Firle Beacon; and so is the pleasure of walking along the ancient ridgeway and looking out over what Kipling called 'the wooded, dim, blue goodness of the Weald'. Even the vast prairie fields have a certain beauty, changing through the year from chalky white to spring green and then to ripe gold. There are still plenty of tracks across the Downs and with very few exceptions these rights of way have been respected, far more so than inland.

The Downs remain miraculously unspoilt when you compare them with the ruined coastal plain nearby. They feel quite primeval in sea-fog or thunderstorm. Even after all these years it is a great joy and privilege to walk over them and I envy anyone who is about to do so for the first time.

Denis Perkins

Walk 1

4 miles (6.5 km)

Queen Elizabeth Country Park and Butser Hill

OS sheet 197

The first walk in the book is not a typical one and lovers of solitude might well prefer to give it a miss, though it is surprising how quickly it is possible to get away from the crowds who flock to the country park, particularly in the summer months, but who, in general, do not stray far from the Park Centre.

I can strongly recommend it as a good family walk, however, with two climbs, but not too long and with plenty to divert the interest of flagging children. A country park leaflet (obtainable from the Park Centre) includes a map showing a number of alternative paths through the Queen Elizabeth Forest and over War Down which will enable you to vary and lengthen the route. The map indicates the Forest and Iron Age demonstration areas which are not included in the written description.

Butser Hill, at 888 feet, is higher than any point on the Sussex Downs. Its prominent radio station makes it a landmark for miles around. It was an Iron Age hill-fort and is now at weekends the scene of various sports and pastimes, including hang-gliding and grass-skiing. The views from the top are not as wide as you might expect because you are looking out on very hilly country, but the church of East Meon provides a prominent landmark to the north-west and the Isle of Wight is visible to the south.

Park at the Queen Elizabeth Country Park Centre car park which is situated to the east of the A3 road about 5 miles south-west of Petersfield (OS map ref. 718184). NB. There is a charge for car parking.

Start the walk by going under the A3 via an underpass. A few yards beyond the main road, turn left off the slip road and follow the way marked 'horse route' up over the shoulder of Butser Hill, aiming for the radio mast on the summit.

Bear round to the right of the radio station and from a triangulation point beyond, keep roughly northwards along the ridge of Ramsdean Down. Go over a stile and follow the right hand side of the hill gently downwards (signposted 'Rake path to Weston'). Cross a stile in the fence line to the right and drop steeply down. Where the open downland narrows to a point near the bottom, go over a stile to the right of a water trough, descend a flight of steps, and go straight across

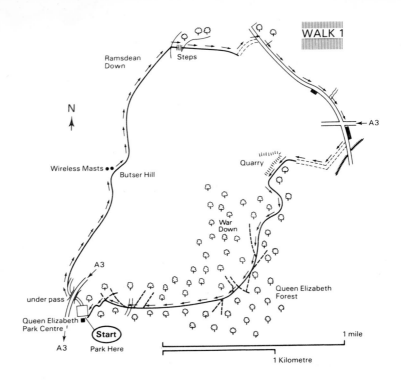

a field and out through a gate on to an access track. Turn left on this track, follow it out to a road and turn right.

Follow this road for $\frac{2}{3}$ mile before crossing the A3 to follow an unclassified road opposite. In about 200 yards, just before a bridge over the railway, turn right on a wide track between hedges. In another 200 yards, immediately after going through a metal field gate, bear right over metal railings into an enclosed track between banks. Follow this for almost $\frac{1}{2}$ mile. Go over a crossing track and in a few yards join a forest ride and keep right uphill. In a few more yards, curve to the left along the perimeter of a quarry area. Now follow this clear wide track up round the side of War Down.

You are now within the afforested area of Queen Elizabeth Country Park and there are a number of paths back to the car park all of which are marked on the map obtainable at the Park Centre. The simplest route will be described here.

In about $\frac{2}{3}$ mile, a few yards after a broad track comes in from the left, fork right slightly downhill. At an open green space where there is a choice of three paths ahead, take the right hand one uphill. Ignore all side tracks and, on meeting a metalled road, go straight across. Ignore the first crossing horse track and in about 250 yards double back to the left on a harder track (signposted Park Centre). Follow this downhill to the car park.

14

Now keep along the right hand edge of a field with more mature conifers to the right. In about 150 yards, go straight across a triangular corner of field and on reaching the hedge at the other side turn left through about 50 degrees and go straight out across an open field aiming towards a bridle gate which you will soon be able to see at the corner of a wood under a large beech tree. Go through this gate and follow a narrow path for about 30 yards before turning left on a wider grassy track. In another 150 yards or so, double back to the left on a well ridden bridleway which soon leaves the wood and follows a broad grassy field headland strip with woodland to the right.

This open strip soon becomes a narrower track between fence and woodland, and then cuts through a corner of woodland. About 50 yards after entering the woodland turn right on a track which leads through Stansted Forest for $\frac{1}{4}$ mile to a road at point A on the sketch map. (Walkers who have used the alternative parking area should start the route description here.)

Turn right along the road and in $\frac{1}{4}$ mile turn left along a clear gravel track. Go straight over several crossing tracks and in 350 yards, at a meeting of five ways, take the 'third exit' (half right). In another 180 yards, turn right on a crossing track for 15 yards only before going sharply left. In 10 yards go over another crossing track and continue on a path which passes between a pit on the left and a large yew tree on the right and on through coppiced woodland. Go straight over a crossing track and descend to leave the forest over wooden railings.

Go slightly right over a field in a dip to cross more wooden railings and climb for a few yards to a crossing track where turn right. Follow this narrow path which soon passes a cottage garden on the left and becomes a wider track which passes an old and overgrown quarry and then a young plantation on the right. Follow this track out to the road at Forestside.

Turn left along the road passing a small church on the left, and in about 50 yards go right over a stile and follow a clear track through woodland. Ignore a swing gate on the left and follow a narrow track eastwards along the edge of woodland. In 200 yards go left over a stile and follow a fence line out to another road.

Turn left along the road for 15 yards before turning right on a wide track. In 250 yards turn right and in another 30 yards keep straight on, ignoring a left turn. Follow this old lane for nearly $\frac{1}{2}$ mile out to a road.

Turn left along the road and in 150 yards turn right (signposted Walderton). In a little over 250 yards turn left over a stile and follow the remains of a hedge line for 400 yards before entering woodland over a stile. Drop down through the woods keeping left at a T-junction after about 100 yards. Follow a path along the side of the hill with views of West Marden opening out through the trees to the right. Finally go over a stile and descend half left across a small paddock which leads you on to a road. Turn right for West Marden and the car.

Walk 3   Harting Downs and North Marden

5½ miles (9 km)

OS sheet 197

This is a varied walk, only a mile or so from the Hampshire border. The early part follows the South Downs Way and looks out over the Rother valley to the sandstone country rising towards Blackdown. There is an Iron Age hill-fort on Beacon Hill. Turning south, the walk goes through some beautiful wooded country, gently undulating and often quite unlike the rest of the Downs.

North Marden is little more than an isolated cluster of church and farm buildings. The church is small and simple – a single room with a most unusual curved chancel wall.

Park at the West Sussex County Council car park and picnic area to the east of the B2141 South Harting to Chichester road on the top of Harting Downs (OS map ref. 790181).

Start off eastwards along the South Downs Way following the ridge of the Downs. In about ⅔ mile, after dropping down into Bramshott Bottom with its elaborate carved oak waypost erected by the Society of Sussex Downsmen, climb steeply to the triangulation point on the top of Beacon Hill at 795 feet.

From this point, on a clear day, there are magnificent views across the Weald with Blackdown to the north and Leith Hill and the North Downs to the north-east. To the east, Ditchling Beacon, over 30 miles away can be picked out if conditions are good, and westwards the ridge of the Downs rises to its highest point at Butser Hill (Walk 1).

After dropping into another dip, go straight ahead over the lower summit of Pen Hill. Continue with the South Downs Way down the other side and, on reaching a belt of conifers, turn right. In 100 yards turn right again on a grassy track which crosses a large field. Follow this track which soon runs between fences. This was once a road from Elsted over the Downs to North Marden. In about ½ mile the path drops down into a valley. A few yards after a path comes in from the left, fork right on a clear track which climbs out of the right side of the valley. Follow this track along the top edge of woodland and then, about 200 yards after a track comes in from the right, turn right on a grassy path which leaves the main track as it turns away to the left. Your path now runs between hedges for just over ¼ mile out to the B2141 road at North Marden.

Turn right along the road and in a little more than 100 yards, turn left. In another 50 yards go right along the access track to North

18

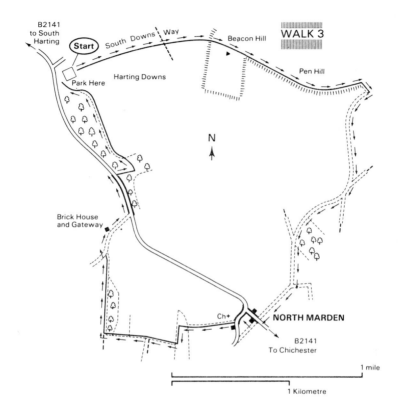

Marden church. After passing the church on your right, go ahead downhill keeping to the left of a line of trees. After crossing two stiles at the bottom, go straight on over a narrow field and turn left along the near side of the hedge ahead. In 100 yards or so turn right over a stile and go ahead (westwards) on a path which is partly within a narrow belt of scrubby woodland. In almost $\frac{1}{2}$ mile, after passing through the left hand end of a plantation of conifers, go over a stile into a field and turn right along the edge of it with woodland to the right, your route being marked by a succession of stiles. After nearly $\frac{1}{2}$ mile join a bridleway coming in from the left and follow it out to the main B2141 road, keeping to the right of a brick lodge and gateway.

This gateway is a back entrance to the Uppark estate, one of the largest in Sussex. There are, unfortunately, no rights of way across the park although some link paths are badly needed. The mansion, built in 1690 in elegant red brick and stone has much of its original 18th century furnishings. It is now in National Trust ownership and is open to the public at certain times during the summer.

For the walker, on reaching the B2141 road, there are more immediate problems of access. Both West Sussex County Council and the landowner have promised a right of way on the opposite side of the road running parallel to it within the woodland. At the time of writing, however, this path has not materialized, and it is therefore necessary to turn left and walk along approximately 350 yards of dangerous road, after which you can turn right on a clear woodland track. About 250 yards along this track, turn left in line with a solitary conifer in the field to your right. Your path meanders through woodland at first and then follows along the left hand edge of an area of rough grassland for $\frac{1}{2}$ mile. Towards the top of the hill turn left on a rutted track into woodland which will take you back to the car park.

Walk 4

Chilgrove and Bow Hill

4 miles (6.5 km)

OS sheet 197

Chilgrove is a delightful spot, consisting of little more than an inn and a few cottages tucked down in a valley and immaculately set beside a green open space.

The short but beautiful walk climbs up from Chilgrove and follows a ridgeway track leading to fine open views from Bow Hill above Kingley Vale. The return route descends over Stoughton Down before climbing back over Chilgrove Hill.

Notes on Bow Hill and Kingley Vale are included under Walk 6. Walks 4 and 6 can be combined to form a total circuit of $9\frac{1}{2}$ miles. The link point is indicated in the route description and on the sketch maps.

For the very energetic a link with Walk 5 is also indicated in the text and on the sketch map. When surveying the paths for inclusion in this book I walked all three on a crisp and sunny day in early April and I cannot recall a finer or more varied downland walk – 16 miles in all.

Park beside the green open space opposite the White Horse Inn at Chilgrove on the B2141 Chichester to South Harting road about 7 miles north of Chichester (OS map ref. 828145).

From the green, cross the B2141 road and follow a flint track up the flank of Chilgrove Hill. Keep to the main track until it levels out at the top of the hill. Here, fork left and follow a rutted track into woodland, soon with yews to the left and a young plantation of conifers to the right. In $\frac{3}{4}$ mile, after passing an isolated cottage on the right, ignore a left fork unless you would like to seek out Goosehill Camp down the hill to the left. It is a circular Iron Age earthwork enclosing half an acre but largely buried in a forest of yews. In its heyday it was possibly a fortified cattle enclosure.

To continue the walk, keep ahead along the ridge of the hill soon reaching a broad forest ride. In about $\frac{1}{2}$ mile fine views open out on the left. Where the path broadens out on to an area of sloping grass downland, keep right (almost straight on) and in about 200 yards at a Kingley Vale Nature Reserve notice and map (the link point with Walk 6) turn back sharply to the right.

In just under 300 yards ignore a bridleway to the left and go ahead through a bridle gate and downhill over Stoughton Down. There are views ahead to Pen Hill and Beacon Hill above the northern scarp of the Downs (included in Walk 3). At a grassy clearing where a number of ways meet, keep straight ahead on the left hand and lower of two

Start Park Here

White Horse
P.H.

B2141 To South Harting

B2141 To Chichester

N

WALK 4

Goosehill Camp

To Walk 5

Stoughton Down

Kingley Vale Nature
Reserve Notice

Bow Hill

Walk 6

1 mile

1 Kilometre

paths, dropping downhill through a beech plantation. In about ½ mile join a roughly metalled track coming in from the right, and in another 300 yards, double sharply back to the right on a broad grassy track. (To link with Walk 5 keep straight on at this point on the hard track for 450 yards.)

Follow the grassy track and, where it forks by a wooden seat, keep left and go through a gate and on up the valley, soon with a line of ancient beeches marking a parish boundary on the left. In ½ mile rejoin your outgoing route and keep straight ahead downhill into Chilgrove.

Walk 5   Up Marden and Stoughton

7 miles (11 km)

OS sheet 197

An up-and-down walk through a wide variety of woodland scenery – not only young plantations of beech but several stretches of mixed woodland, some coppiced, some left wild and overgrown. A link with Walk 4 is indicated in the text and on the sketch map.

Up Marden is a tiny and remote hamlet high up in the Downs, little more than a farm and church adjoining.

Stoughton is an attractive village with a pub in a valley running down towards the Hampshire border.

East Marden is a compact flint and tile village in a hollow, with a characteristic little downland church and a village pump with a round thatched roof. It is not quite on the described walk but, allowing an extra mile, is well worth a short detour, either by footpath or along the road, both of which are indicated on the sketch map.

Park at the Stoughton Down Forestry Commission car parking area. This can be reached by turning right (eastwards) off the B2146 Chichester to Petersfield road at Walderton, about 7 miles north-west of Chichester. In 1 mile go through Stoughton and the car park is on the right, on a corner, about $1\frac{1}{4}$ miles further on up the valley (OS map ref. 815127).

On leaving the car park, turn right along the road. In about 300 yards, opposite a Forestry Commission notice 'Wildham Wood', turn left along an access drive, pass to the right of a house and climb within the left hand edge of woodland. Ignore all side turnings and climb through mature beeches at first and then on through a younger beech plantation. On leaving the wood, immediately turn right along the edge of it with a field on your left. At the end of the field, go straight ahead into woods again and descend to a road. (To visit East Marden take the field path which starts from this point as indicated on the sketch map.)

To continue the described walk turn left along the road for $\frac{1}{4}$ mile and then, about 50 yards before the road passes under power lines, turn left on a track into woods. Follow this track along the foot of the slope within the edge of the wood for another $\frac{1}{4}$ mile and then, at an oblique crossing track, turn left, steeply uphill. At the top of the wood go over a stile and keep straight ahead along the left hand edge of a field to join a road.

Turn left along the road for 100 yards before turning right on a farm

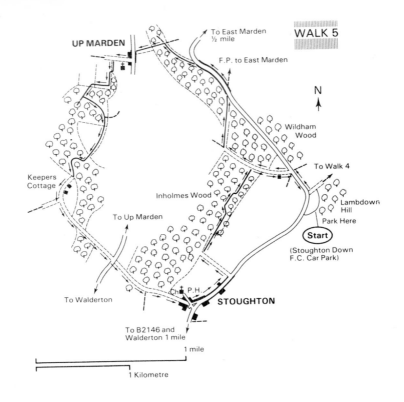

UP MARDEN

To East Marden
½ mile

F.P. to East Marden

N

Wildham
Wood

Keepers
Cottage

To Walk 4

Inholmes Wood

Lambdown
Hill

To Up Marden

Park Here

Start

(Stoughton Down
F.C. Car Park)

To Walderton

P.H.

STOUGHTON

To B2146 and
Walderton 1 mile

1 mile

1 Kilometre

track. Access to Up Marden church is obtained from this track on the
left. The 13th century church of St. Michael, Up Marden, is small,
simple and candle-lit, with white walls and a brick floor. The wooden
bell turret can no longer bear the weight of the three 17th century
bells. Two of them stand on the chancel floor and the third has been
hung by the porch outside.

Continue along the farm track and about 80 yards beyond the
church turn left over a stile and follow a field edge to find and cross
another stile on the right at the corner of a wood. Drop downhill
following the left hand edge of the next field round and, at the bottom
corner, go over another stile and ascend along the left hand edge of a
third field. About half way up go over a stile on the left into woods. In
50 yards turn left, downhill, and at the bottom keep straight on, ignoring a right fork, and climb. At a T-junction turn right and descend,
following the path out of the wood and along the left hand edge of a
large field. At the bottom corner of this field continue ahead into
woodland again and follow the main track which curves right, then

24

left and uphill through the wood. Towards the top cross over an oblique crossing track and emerge from the wood to pass two cottages on your left.

Soon after passing the second cottage (Keepers Cottage) keep straight on at a T-junction on a tree-lined path which soon enters woodland. Ignore all crossing tracks and descend to cross a road in the valley.

Go straight across the road and ahead up the left hand edge of a field. After passing under power lines, follow a clear track half left into woods and uphill. Once again, ignore all side tracks and follow the main path for $\frac{2}{3}$ mile into Stoughton village. The church is on the left just before reaching the road in the village and is well worth visiting. Some of the original Saxon work remains including an impressive chancel arch.

At the road turn left, passing the Hare and Hounds public house on the left and in about 600 yards (about 200 yards beyond the last house on the left), turn left on an enclosed track which climbs towards a belt of woodland. Just short of the woods, turn right over a stile and follow along the edge of the wooded area with views across the valley to Bow Hill. At the corner of the field go straight ahead over a stile into the wood. Your path now keeps approximately along the contour in the same general direction (north-northeast) for $\frac{3}{4}$ mile. The path meanders through the wood a good deal and does not coincide with the right of way as mapped by the Ordnance Survey, but you can't go wrong if you aim to keep at about the same height along the valley, finally joining your outgoing route and turning right to descend to the road. Here turn right and return to the car park.

(To link with Walk 4 go through a field gate at the northern corner of the car park and follow a roughly metalled track for 450 yards round the shoulder of Lambdown Hill.)

Walk 6 Kingley Vale

4 or 5½ miles (6.5 or 9 km)

OS sheet 197

This is a fairly short walk through what has been described as 'the finest yew forest in Europe', and climbing to the top of Bow Hill with fine views into Hampshire and across the Chichester creeks to the sea and the Isle of Wight. The walk can be extended by linking it with Walk 4 as indicated in the route description.

Kingley Vale is now protected by the Nature Conservancy Council. It is an area of great beauty and interest, and not only to naturalists. A section of the walk follows part of a Nature Trail passing the oldest yew trees, now 500 years old, and then climbing up through the younger part of the forest where the trees are up to 100 years old, offspring of the ancient yews in the valley.

Bow Hill is a very ancient spot. On the top four Bronze Age barrows, known as the Devil's Humps, stand beside an ancient trackway – two bell barrows to the south-west, which are visible for miles around, and two bowl barrows to the north-east. The whole area is rich in earthworks, including an Iron Age farmstead and possibly some Neolithic flint mines.

Park at the Kingley Vale car park which is situated on the unclassified road to the north of East Ashling and west of West Stoke. To reach it turn right (north) off the B2178 Chichester to Petersfield road where it makes a sharp right-angled turn in the village of East Ashling 3 miles north-west of Chichester (OS map ref. 820079). The car park is on the right in ¾ mile, just beyond a road junction at OS map ref. 824087.

From the car park go over a stile by a metal gate and follow a roughly metalled track for ¾ mile to the foot of Kingley Vale. Keep straight on, passing to the left of the Field Centre (well worth a visit if open) and follow part of the signposted and numbered Nature Trail (for which a very well produced guide is available from a dispenser) for another ¾ mile to the top of Bow Hill with its two prominent bell barrows. Go right up to these two mounds on the summit before doubling back to the right along the top of the hill, passing immediately to the right of two more barrows and a flint viewpoint table. There are fine views northwards to the Downs escarpment from Linch Down to Butser Hill and southwards to Chichester and the Isle of Wight.

Follow a clear track eastwards and, soon after passing a triangulation point on your left, turn right downhill on a crossing track by a

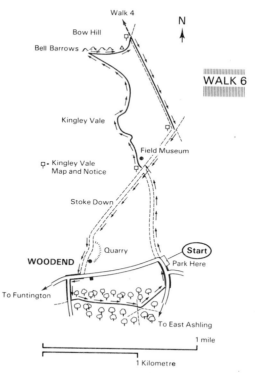

Nature Reserve notice (this is the link point for Walk 4). Drop down on a sunken track from which there are views ahead to Stoke Clump and Chichester cathedral beyond. At the bottom of the hill, after passing another Nature Reserve notice, go straight ahead with a fence on your right. In just over $\frac{1}{4}$ mile turn right at a crossing track and follow it back to cross your outgoing route at the foot of Kingley Vale. (To return directly to the car park on the 4 mile walk, turn left here.)

To continue the $5\frac{1}{2}$ mile walk, keep straight ahead past another Nature Reserve notice and follow a path between fences over the shoulder of Stoke Down and downhill past an old quarry for nearly a mile to reach the road at Woodend.

At the road turn right, and in 100 yards turn left. Ignore the first track into woodland on the left but after another 180 yards, where a track crosses the road, turn left through a gate and follow a straight woodland path. Ignore all side tracks for $\frac{1}{2}$ mile and then, about 50 yards beyond a wide crossing track (signposted at the time of writing), fork left on an oblique crossing track, follow this out to a road and turn left. In 150 yards at a T-junction, turn left and return to the car park.

27

Walk 7   Singleton and East Dean

6½ miles (10.5 km)

OS sheet 197

Goodwood is often claimed to be the most picturesque racecourse in the British Isles. Although it would certainly be wise to avoid attempting this walk on a race day, at other times the course, set 500 feet up into the Downs, is as good a place as any to begin a downland walk. This one starts by climbing to the Trundle, an impressive Iron Age hill-fort encircling the summit of St. Roche's Hill, so called because it was the site of a medieval chapel. From the top, there are magnificent views across the coastal plain towards the sea with the Isle of Wight on the horizon. In the foreground can be seen the spire of Chichester cathedral and the shining pattern of the creeks of Chichester harbour stretched out towards Hayling Island.

The walk continues by descending to the neat and prosperous looking village of Singleton. From here a short detour from the described route will take you to the Weald and Downland open air museum. This is a unique collection of old buildings, mostly rescued from almost certain destruction on their original sites in various parts of southern England, and painstakingly re-erected on the spacious museum site in West Dean park. One building, Bayleaf, is a superb 15th century hall from the Weald, and other exhibits include a 14th century farmhouse and a 19th century toll cottage. A charcoal burners' camp has been reconstructed as part of a woodland nature trail.

After climbing over Levin Down and Court Hill, the walk descends to the small village of East Dean, set, like Singleton, in a downland valley. The final climb through East Dean park brings you back to Goodwood.

Park in the large car parking area at Goodwood country park which is situated immediately to the south of Goodwood racecourse. To get there, turn north off the A27 Chichester to Arundel road at Westhampnett, a mile east of Chichester. Turn right just before reaching the racecourse buildings. The car park is on the right after passing the grandstand (OS map ref. 885110).

From the car park follow the road westwards past the grandstand. At a T-junction (signposted Singleton and Midhurst) turn right. In 300 yards turn left on a chalky track which passes to the left of a race-course area called the Trundle Enclosure, and climb with metal railings on your right. Where the bridleway curves away to the left round

28

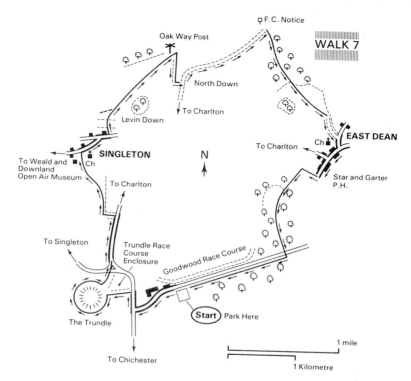

the flank of the hill, take a footpath which keeps close to the railings and climbs to the Trundle on the top. After encircling the ramparts, preferably in a clockwise direction to obtain all the available views, drop down northwards with metal railings on your right and go straight across a triangular parking area to follow a narrow road into the valley.

In about ½ mile turn left at a stile. (The true line of this path leaves the road about 300 yards farther up the hill but is obstructed and is the subject of legal dispute. Unless otherwise signposted it is therefore best, for the time being, to use the stiled route.) After crossing the stile, go westwards between fences for 150 yards before turning right with the fence on your right and following it into the valley heading for Singleton church which is finally reached through a very muddy farmyard. Go round the church in a clockwise direction within the churchyard wall and exit to the road by the Fox and Hounds public house in Singleton village. (To visit the Weald and Downland open air museum turn left here.)

To continue the walk, turn right along the road. At a junction keep straight on, signposted Charlton and East Dean, and in 150 yards, immediately after crossing the Lavant stream, turn left between school and graveyard and climb up on to Levin Down, in the second

29

field going slightly right to a stile which can be seen in the hedge on the skyline. A few yards beyond this hedge, go right on a bridleway which curves rather indistinctly round the left flank of Levin Down (ignore a signposted crossing track). Beyond a field gate there is little to guide you, but you should follow the side of the hill round, staying approximately at the same contour level, eventually walking parallel to and about 200 yards away from a belt of woodland to the left. Now aim downhill for a substantial carved oak waypost ahead and at the post turn right, signposted Charlton. Follow a clear chalk track downhill with Levin Down now rising steeply up on the right. At the bottom curve left with the path and in 50 yards, at a T-junction, turn left.

Now follow this clear flint track, North Lane, which curves round the flank of North Down to the right and continues up the floor of a valley for more than $\frac{1}{2}$ mile. At a Forestry Commission notice 'Charlton Forest' and five yards short of a gate, turn right on a narrow path, over a stile, and along the left hand edge of a short section of open downland before climbing through woods. Go through a bridle gate and continue to climb on a grassy track through a plantation of conifers. Go straight over two wide grassy rides before entering deciduous woodland and going straight over a crossing track. At the top edge of the woodland the footpath keeps straight on over the open downland, but if it is ploughed and planted it may be easiest to follow the often well trodden path round the left hand side of the field along the edge of the woodland. After crossing a stile, where the edge of the woodland drops away more steeply to the left, keep straight on over the open downland, soon veering gradually left towards a line of trees down the hill on your left. (At the time of writing the path is obstructed by a barbed wire fence but negotiations are in hand to provide a stile.) Converge on the line of trees at a stile and gate and go ahead with the line of trees to the left, now on a clear track which soon descends in a hollow way between banks. Follow this round to the left, down to a road and turn right.

In a little over 100 yards, turn right at a T-junction and descend into East Dean village. After passing the Star and Garter public house, ignore a turning to the left, and after passing a pond on the right, fork left (signposted to Goodwood and Chichester). Climb out of the village and in about 250 yards, immediately after passing under power lines, fork right on a chalky track. Follow a fence line which keeps parallel to the power lines, soon joining a track between fences. In 150 yards go left through a barbed wire gate and climb the shoulder of Park Hill converging on a fence to the right and entering a wooded area. Keep on the left hand side of an open area on the top of the hill, mostly within the trees on a fairly clear track, then through a wooden field gate to follow a clearer track through a more substantial area of woodland and out to a road. Turn right at the road and return along it for $\frac{3}{4}$ mile to the car park. There is room to walk within the strip of woodland to the left of the road.

This is a walk which, unlike any other in the book, confines itself to an area immediately to the north of the Downs. It offers fine views of the wooded northern slopes and includes a section along the foot of the escarpment. The walk begins and ends in the middle of the belt of heathland which runs parallel to the Downs, a few miles inland, from the River Adur westwards. This is sandy, heather and pine country, infertile but very beautiful and in complete contrast to the Downs themselves.

Graffham is a long, straggling village which ends at the foot of the Downs with some picturesque old houses clustered round a much restored grey flint church with a fine spire.

Park at Lavington Common. To get there turn left (west) off the A285 Chichester–Petworth road about a mile north of Duncton, signposted Graffham and Selham. The parking area is on the right after about $1\frac{1}{2}$ miles, by a National Trust notice 'Lavington Common' (OS map ref. 949187).

On leaving the car park, turn left for a few yards along the road and then go right through a gate with the top bar partly painted green. Keep straight ahead on a clear track through a plantation of conifers. In about 250 yards, ignore a wide track to the right and go ahead between wooden posts. In a further 250 yards, ignore another ride to the right. After leaving the planted area and passing a red brick house on the right, turn right at a T-junction and follow a roughly metalled track through farm buildings. A few yards beyond the last building on the left, turn left with the main track, walking due south towards the Downs.

In about 300 yards, immediately beyond a strip of woodland on the right, turn right along the edge of the trees with two wooden bungalows to the left. Go over a stile and follow a narrow path through a wooded area and out, over another stile, to a road on which you should keep right. In about 100 yards, where the road bends to the right, keep straight on along a hard access track. Immediately beyond a house on the left, go left over a stile and in 100 yards left over a second stile to continue southwards on the other side of the hedge. After a short enclosed section of path between hedge and wooden fence, join a hard track and follow it southwards with paddocks to the left and passing the buildings of Lavington Stud Farm.

31

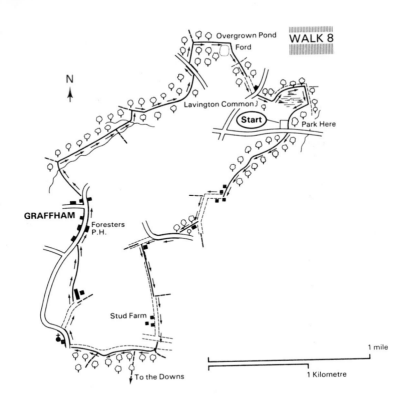

On reaching the foot of the Downs, keep straight ahead at a T-junction over a narrow strip of pasture to cross a stile into woodland. Immediately beyond the stile, fork right and, in about 100 yards, at an oblique crossing track, keep right and climb to join another track coming in from behind on the left. The more energetic can now climb to the top of the Downs through a bridle gate on the left, but the walk continues westwards along the foot of the escarpment. Ignore the next left fork, uphill through a field gate, and keep to the main track. At a meeting of a number of ways in a more open area turn right downhill on the chalky track. In a few yards there is a good view northwards to Petworth. Follow the track to the road at Graffham church.

Immediately opposite the church, fork right on a private road to Lavington Stud (it is a public footpath) and in 300 yards keep to the left of some buildings on a grassy strip with wooden railings to the left. Go through gaps in two sets of railings and continue ahead on a wide green strip between fence and hedge, subsequently crossing an open field on a well trodden, slightly raised, grassy path to join the road at Graffham by a war memorial.

Follow the road north through the village, passing the Foresters' inn. Ignore the left turn, signposted to Selham, and in less than 100 yards, opposite a bungalow called High View, fork left on a track between hedges, in 50 yards going ahead through a metal field gate. Now, follow a dirt track along the left hand edge of the first field and on through two more gates with stiles beside them. Beyond the second gate go diagonally left downhill across an open field to two bridle gates and a stream crossing into woodland. Climb for 50 yards beyond the stream and then, at a T-junction, turn right on a narrow track. Shortly, bear right past a large dilapidated shed and follow a most beautiful path through woodland with a stream below you on the right. Ignore minor tracks to right and left and, after passing through a rhododendron thicket, drop down to the stream bank and keep left, following the stream. Do not go over a footbridge to the right but follow a narrow path, still with the stream on your right for about 300 yards before bearing left to cross a plank bridge over a tributary stream. About 100 yards beyond the bridge, turn right on a heavily ridden sandy track. Follow this clear track across Graffham Common, now planted with conifers. Ignore all side tracks and in $\frac{1}{2}$ mile pass a house and join a road.

Turn left along the road for about 100 yards and then turn right on a well ridden track through rhododendrons. In 300 yards, turn right at a T-junction and follow a wider track. In $\frac{1}{4}$ mile turn right over a ford by a broken bridge, and follow another clear track for $\frac{1}{3}$ mile to a road.

From this point the easiest, but least interesting, way back to the car park is to turn right and then left at a cross roads. But ahead of you lies the National Trust area of Lavington Common and it is well worthwhile trying to find a way back across it. There are several possibilities. You can get on to the common by going a few yards to the left on the road before turning right on a clear path into the woods. Ignore minor side tracks and follow the main path out on to open heathland. From the edge of the open area, the car park lies almost due south towards the Downs, but there is no direct path. If you would prefer not to strike out across the trackless heath, which is boggy in places, follow a wide sandy track eastwards along the edge of the open area with young conifers to the left. On reaching a plantation of larger trees, turn right for 300 yards only before taking a narrow winding path to the right (south-west) which meanders back to the car parking area.

Walk 9   Stane Street

9 miles (13 km)

OS sheet 197

This is one of the longer and more strenuous walks through undulating and mainly wooded downland. It includes a $2\frac{1}{2}$ mile stretch of Roman road as well as some pleasant sheltered forest rides through young Forestry Commission beechwoods and an open section across Selhurst Park with views to the coastal plain. A waymarked Forestry Commission forest trail starts from the car park at the beginning of the walk. Walks 9 and 10 may be linked as indicated in the route description to give an energetic 18-mile circuit.

Park at the Forestry Commission car park at Eartham Wood which is reached by forking left off the A285 Petworth to Chichester road about 4 miles south of Duncton and 7 miles north-east of Chichester. The large parking area is on the left in less than $\frac{1}{2}$ mile from the turn-off (OS map ref. 939106).

From the car park take a narrow track which runs parallel to the road and leaves the car park from the first 'bay' on the right inside the entrance. In about 150 yards turn left along a roughly metalled track which follows the line of Stane Street. Continue through Eartham Wood for about a mile. At a meeting of six bridleways where there is a substantial carved oak way-post, keep straight on out of the forest area to follow one of the best preserved sections of the Roman road.

Stane Street linked London and Chichester and is clearly visible as it crosses the Downs between Bignor Hill and the A285 road below Halnaker Hill, aligned with the spire of Chichester cathedral. Now covered with grass, the *agger* was built with a foundation of rammed flint and chalk capped with flint and gravel. Traces of the drainage ditches on either side can be seen in a few places.

After about $\frac{3}{4}$ mile and fairly soon after passing Gumber Farm away to the right, footpath and bridleway divide and run parallel. It is pleasanter to keep left on the footpath which follows the line of the Roman *agger* and is narrow in places. Finally, immediately after crossing a stile, go sharp left and follow a clear track westwards for a mile. (To link with Walk 10 keep straight on along Stane Street to the top of Bignor Hill.)

Keep going westwards on the track which has been churned up by timber hauling, until, about 60 yards short of a Forestry Commission notice 'Eartham Wood', you should turn right. In a few yards only fork left and very shortly fork right, to pass through a planted area,

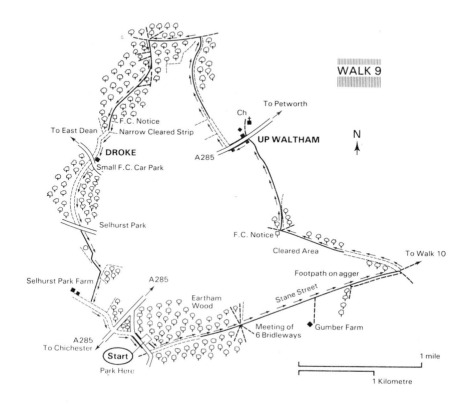

To Petworth

Ch

To East Dean

F.C. Notice

Narrow Cleared Strip

UP WALTHAM

N

DROKE

A285

Small F.C. Car Park

Selhurst Park

F.C. Notice

Cleared Area

To Walk 10

Selhurst Park Farm

A285

Footpath on agger

Stane Street

Eartham
Wood

A285
To Chichester

Meeting of
6 Bridleways

Gumber Farm

Start

Park Here

1 mile

1 Kilometre

now heading north. Soon the path follows along the right hand edge of a field with forestry plantation to the right, and then continues across open downland descending into the valley at Upwaltham, joining the A285 road through farm buildings.

Upwaltham is a tiny flint and tile hamlet with a lovely little downland church, simple and basically unaltered since the 13th century. Cardinal Manning, the Roman Catholic Archbishop of Westminster in late Victorian times, was rector here before 'changing sides'.

To visit the church, which was until fairly recently lit by candles in chandeliers, go straight across the road and take a track immediately to the left of a square flint building. But to continue the walk turn left along the A285 for about 250 yards, and then, just beyond a cottage on the left, go right over a stile and climb, in a hollow way at first, on to Waltham Down. Beyond the hollow section, keep along the left hand edge of a field at first and then along the meandering right hand edge of a large field for about $\frac{3}{4}$ mile, with woodland dropping away to the right.

At the top corner of this field do not take the first track to the right but curve to the left with the edge of the field for a few yards only before turning right on a rough track. In another few yards turn left on a wider track which soon opens out to become a broad fire break. In a little over $\frac{1}{4}$ mile, at a clearing where a number of ways meet, turn left on a clear track. In another $\frac{1}{4}$ mile where the main track curves left, fork right, soon joining a broader track coming in from the left. Follow this forest track downhill, continuing straight on when the main track forks right, and soon passing a Forestry Commission notice to cross a narrow strip of open land, then descending through a wooded area to the road at Droke.

Turn left along the road for about 100 yards before going right, immediately short of a car parking area. Now ignore all side tracks and climb for nearly half a mile through an afforested area to the Selhurst Park road. Go straight across the road and over a stile, then strike out diagonally left across Selhurst Park, aiming for an isolated group of trees which includes a large evergreen oak.

There are fine views over the coastal plain and across to the prominent hilltop landmark of Halnaker Mill, a solid brick tower structure, built in 1750, restored in 1934, and still with sweeps and fantail.

About 60 yards beyond the isolated group of trees turn right (in the middle of the field) and aim towards a gate and the buildings of Selhurst Park farm beyond. Do not go through the gate but turn left a few yards short of it and aim for a stile at the right hand end of a line of woodland. Beyond the stile, turn south again and pass three isolated trees to join Selhurst Park farm access track. Turn left along this and follow it out to the A285 road.

Go straight across the road, continue on a clear track through to another road and turn right to return to the car park.

Walk 10

Bignor Hill and Barlavington

9 miles (13 km)

OS sheet 197

This is a fairly long but very fine walk which starts off through the
Forestry Commission area of Houghton Forest but then climbs to the
top of Bignor Hill before following a splendid section along the edge of
the Downs escarpment inexplicably eschewed by the planners of the
official South Downs Way in favour of a much inferior route further to
the south. The return journey traverses the foothills of the Downs and
passes through the villages of Sutton and Bignor (with an opportunity
to visit the Roman villa) before climbing back over Westburton Hill.
This walk may be combined with Walk 9 to give a combined circuit of
18 miles.

Park in the large car park at Whiteways Lodge at the junction of the
A29 and A284 roads about 3 miles north of Arundel (OS map ref.
001109).

Leave the car park along a track about 50 yards to the right of the
refreshment kiosk. Go straight ahead past a Forestry Commission
notice 'Houghton Forest' and on through a bridle gate. In about 500
yards keep left and then ignore all turnings to right and left for just
over a mile. Leave the forest through a bridle gate and go ahead, now
with an open field on your right and a plantation to the left. Towards
the end of this field the path crosses the site of Barkhale, a Neolithic
causewayed camp – one of only four in the South Downs area, the
other three being at the Trundle, Goodwood (Walk 7), Coombe Hill,
Jevington (Walk 30) and Whitehawk, Brighton. Barkhale has been
largely obliterated by ploughing.

Where the field on the right ends, turn right on a crossing track and
ascend to the National Trust open space at Bignor Post. You are now
at over 700 feet above sea level and there are fine views northwards
over the Weald and eastwards along the Downs to Chanctonbury
Ring and Wolstonbury Hill beyond. The Roman road Stane Street
crosses the line of the walk a little to the west of this point and the sign-
post on the summit reminds us that it was the direct route from
Londinium to Regnum (Chichester).

From Bignor Post follow the South Downs Way westwards on a
chalky track aiming towards two radio masts and in about 200 yards
keep right, crossing the line of Stane Street. (To link with Walk 9 turn
left and follow the line of Stane Street.)

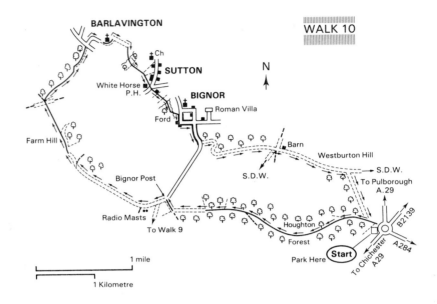

Pass to the right of the radio masts, soon ignoring a left turn and beginning to drop downhill. In just under ½ mile and a few yards before the main track curves away to the left (not a right of way), turn right through an area of scrub, and in about 30 yards, where the track divides into three, keep to the leftmost fork. Your path now follows a line of trees and then curves to the right along the top edge of woodland on the right and the flank of Farm Hill on the left. Ignore a right fork which follows the edge of the woodland downhill and instead keep straight ahead on a track which crosses open downland and drops down over a large field. Go over a crossing track, ignore the first track on the right into woods in 30 yards, but 10 yards further on fork right on a clear grassy bridleway. This fine terraced path drops down into the valley at Barlavington. Towards the bottom the official bridle route keeps outside the woodland to the right, but pedestrians may go over a stile and are normally permitted to use the fine hollow way which drops down within the woodland.

At the bottom go straight across a road and follow the access road to Barlavington church, a simple 13th century structure beside a farmyard with a fine view of the thickly wooded Downs.

Take a footpath which keeps round to the south of the church within the churchyard. After leaving the churchyard, skirt some farm buildings on a clear track and then turn right, at first with park railings on your right and a line of conifers to the left and then on a grass track between hedges. Near the bottom of the hill go over a stile in the hedge on your right and descend across a meadow skirting to the right of a partially dried up pond, to cross a stream by a stone bridge. In 10 yards keep right and climb up through a narrow belt of woodland and over a stile into a field.

Now ascend along the left hand edge of this field, ignoring a path off to the left about two-thirds of the way up, and where the ground levels out strike out half left on a path which is usually trodden out through the crop. (To visit Sutton's 12th to 14th century church with its fine shingled cap, turn left instead of going diagonally across the field – to rejoin the walk turn right on the road through the village to the White Horse public house.) At the far side of the field go over a stile and pick up a narrow path which leads to the road at the White Horse.

At the road turn right and in a few yards at a T-junction go almost straight ahead on a path to the right of a thatched cottage and out into a field. Go straight out across this field, downhill, through a metal field gate and on to a wooden gate and a bridge over a stream. Now keep left on a winding track through woodland. Recross the stream by a ford and climb to a road. Turn right along the road and follow it round to the left through the village of Bignor. Alternatively, to see the best of the village turn left and follow the 'square' of roads round as shown on the sketch map. Bignor is a village with two famous buildings – The Old Shop, a much photographed 15th century cottage at the eastern end of the village, and one of the largest Roman Villas in England. This was uncovered by the plough in 1811, first excavated in 1827, and contains some magnificent tessellated pavement in beautifully clear colours. Its location is also indicated on the sketch map.

Leave the village along the road to the Downs. If you have not made a detour to visit the village or the villa, it is simply a matter, having climbed to the road from the ford, of turning right, following the road round to the left and in 200 yards turning right at a crossroads. Follow the road to the Downs past a farm and upwards for about $\frac{1}{4}$ mile. Where the road turns fairly sharply to the right, go straight ahead on a bridleway, in 50 yards keeping right to follow the main track upwards for something over $\frac{1}{2}$ mile, finally descending to join the South Downs Way. Here, go straight ahead passing to the right of three adjacent barns and climb over the flank of Westburton Hill with fine views opening out to Highdown Hill (Walk 15) and the sea beyond.

In about a mile the path converges on woodland to the right. Where this woodland ends, turn right and follow a clear track with a fence on your left and a belt of woodland on your right. In $\frac{2}{3}$ mile cut through the corner of woodland to pick up and rejoin the outgoing route at the entrance to Houghton Forest. Turn left and return to the car park.

Walk 11   Slindon Woods

5½ miles (9 km)

OS sheet 197

The magnificent beeches of Slindon Park provide the main feature of this pleasant downland walk which passes through a small part of the Slindon estate of 3503 acres which the National Trust inherited under the will of Mr F. Wooton Isaacson in 1950. The estate stretches to the northern foot of the Downs beyond Bignor Hill and Glatting Beacon.

Slindon is a well-kept village, most of which also belongs to the National Trust. It contains many attractive flint cottages and a much restored church with a splendid carved wooden effigy of a 16th century knight in armour, the only one like it in Sussex.

The Sussex poet and author Hilaire Belloc was born here.

A link with Walk 12 to give a combined length of 11 miles is indicated in the description and on the map.

Park in the National Trust car park at the entrance to Slindon Woods on the A29 road about 300 yards north of its junction with the A27 at Fontwell, 4 miles west of Arundel (OS map ref. 953072).

From the car parking area go through the castellated entrance to Slindon Park and keep straight ahead along a gravel track. In 250 yards fork left with the main track and keep on this for about ½ mile. Just after passing through a field gate, double back sharply to the left downhill, then in 150 yards turn right and in another 75 yards right again to follow a clear path out to a road.

At the road turn left and in about 100 yards turn right on an enclosed bridleway which climbs for more than a mile to the top of Nore Hill. The building which you can see on the hill away to the right as you climb is Nore Folly, built as a summer house and apparently intended for shooting lunches. It is now a ruin. Ignore all side turnings and keep to the main track which has been badly eroded by horses in places and can be very muddy. Towards the top a view to the north begins to open out on the left of the path. Keep going until you get to a clear rutted track on which you should turn sharply back to the left, dropping down into the valley. At the first crossing track turn right and in about 200 yards right again at a T-junction. In 60 yards keep left and follow a clear track out to a farm road by a National Trust notice. Here turn right.

After just under ¼ mile along the road fork left along a dirt track through a narrow belt of woodland and out into a field. Follow the fence line up the left hand edge of this field and keep straight on

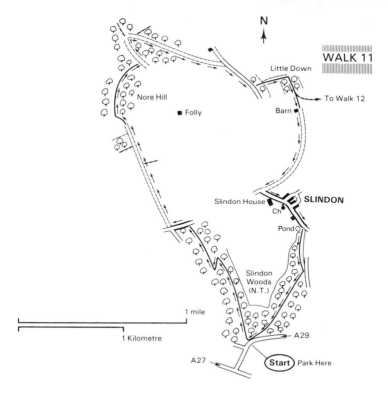

through a strip of woodland. At the far side of the wooded strip turn right and follow a wide track within the left hand edge of the wooded area.

(To link with Walk 12 soon bear left with the fence line on your left and in 100 yards turn left, signposted 'Bridle road to Bignor', on a clear path across a large field.)

To continue with this walk, however, keep right following the main track and passing a barn on the right after 200 yards. Now follow this track for nearly $\frac{1}{2}$ mile out to a road and turn left, soon passing Slindon House on your right.

Slindon House was once a palace of the Archbishops of Canterbury. Of the original palace only a stump of a tower remains. The house was rebuilt in 1560 and again in 1921. It is now a school.

In the centre of the village fork right soon passing Slindon church on the right. Immediately after passing a pond on the right, turn sharp right along the edge of the pond and enter Slindon Woods by a National Trust notice. Just inside the woods, where the path forks, keep left and follow a clear track to a small parking area. Just short of the road at the entrance to this car park, turn right past some wooden railings on a broad track which leads back through the woods to the start of the walk.

41

A walk through thickly wooded downland and visiting the attractive village of Slindon (see Walk 11). There is a fine open stretch over Little Down.

Madehurst is a tiny hamlet beautifully set in wooded country at the end of a cul-de-sac. The name means 'Speech Wood', probably because the Moot, an early form of local government was held in the parish at a spot called Nonemanneslond ('No man's land'), recorded in 1361.

The church looks interesting but is largely a Victorian rebuilding, with a Norman west door. It contains a number of memorials to the family who lived in the great house (demolished in 1959) of nearby Dale Park.

Fairmile Bottom is a wide and beautiful valley, somewhat marred by the busy A29 road running through it. West Sussex County Council owns and manages a 120 acre public open space and picnic area on the south-east side of the valley, partly open grassland and partly beech and yew woodland. A mile-long Nature Trail starts from the same point as this walk (though it follows a different route) and is laid out with 17 numbered stopping places. If you would like to add it to the beginning or end of the walk, an informative leaflet guide is available from a dispenser at the beginning of the trail.

Walks 11 and 12 can be combined to form a figure-of-eight circuit of 11 miles (or 12 with the Nature Trail). Details of the short link between the walks is given in the route description.

Park behind the Fairmile Bottom Cafe (OS map ref. 991097) on the south-east side of the A29 about 3 miles north-east of Fontwell.

The Nature Trail follows a circular route up the valley, but to follow the described walk, start from the cafe by walking *down* the valley in a south-westerly direction keeping parallel to the A29 and traversing the Fairmile Bottom open space. There is no obvious path at first but it is soon possible to follow a well ridden path along an increasingly open grassy slope still parallel to but well above the road. After about ½ mile look out for a crossing track which starts from the road by a white notice board. Turn left on this track which climbs steeply out of the valley through some yews. Near the top of the hill go over a crossing track and in about 150 yards, at a point where six ways meet, take the first path to the right and keep to the main track through Rewell

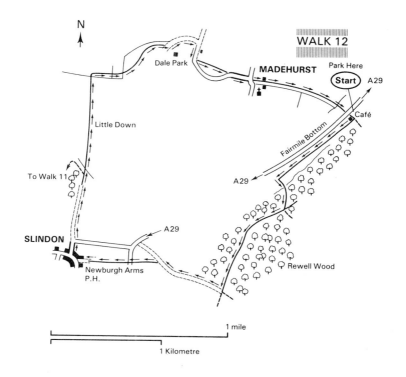

N

WALK 12

Dale Park

MADEHURST

Park Here

Start A29

Café

Little Down

Fairmile Bottom

To Walk 11

A29

A29

SLINDON

Newburgh Arms
P.H.

Rewell Wood

1 mile

1 Kilometre

Wood, ignoring all side tracks for ¾ mile. The wood is full of earthworks which have been the subject of much archaeological speculation. It may have been the site of a sort of Celtic city.

At a meeting of five ways turn right (just north of west) downhill, ignoring a left turn in 75 yards. In the valley where a number of paths join, keep straight on along the main track, but where the main path starts to climb gently, take a narrower path which forks to the left. In 50 yards go over a stile into a field. Go straight ahead across this field and over three more stiles to reach the main A29 road.

Go straight across the road and up some steps to follow a clear path to the Newburgh Arms public house in Slindon. At the road keep right past the Post Office and in 100 yards turn right. In another 250 yards where the road goes right keep straight ahead on a rutted track which climbs at first and then drops down through a belt of woodland. Towards the bottom of the woodland fork right and cross an open piece of ground to a gate leading into a large field. (To link with Walk 11 do not go through this gate but bear left with a fence on your right for about 100 yards before doubling back to the left on a wide track.)

43

To continue with Walk 12 go through the gate and follow a clear track, signposted 'Bridle Road to Bignor', across the middle of the large open area of Little Down, marked with black and white way-posts. In about $\frac{2}{3}$ mile, immediately beyond a line of trees, turn right and follow the field edge down into a dip, over two stiles and up again. At the top, go through a metal field gate and strike out half left across the next field, converging on a fence line on your left and following it to a gate in the top left hand corner of the field.

Immediately beyond this gate turn sharp left on a hard track which curves to the right and soon joins a metalled road. Follow this to a T-junction where turn right. About 100 yards beyond a flint cottage on the left your path breaks off the road to the left through a belt of woodland and over a stile into a field. Follow a line of three cedar trees downhill across this field and rejoin the metalled road in the bottom corner. (NB. West Sussex County Council seeks to divert this section of the path on to the road. The matter is disputed and the result of a public inquiry is awaited. If you find the field path blocked off and the road route signposted, please use it as it will mean that the diversion has been officially confirmed.)

From the bottom corner of the field follow the road uphill bearing right at a junction to reach the tiny hamlet of Madehurst. Just beyond a telephone box where the road turns right keep straight on along a rough track which leads into a field over a stile. Keep along the right hand edge of this field and the next, dropping down into Fairmile Bottom and climbing again to the A29 and the start of the walk.

Walk 13   Perry Hill and Burpham

6½ miles (9.5 km)

OS sheet 197

This is a fine open downland walk, starting at a height of over 600 feet and dropping down to less than 100 feet in the Arun valley. There are superb views across the river to Arundel Park and beyond where the Downs become more wooded for the last 18 miles or so to the Hampshire border.

Burpham is an unspoilt village at the end of a lane which goes nowhere else. The name, from the Old English *Burh Ham*, means a 'settlement by a stronghold', and earthworks to the south of the church are the remains of the Saxon fort built by King Alfred to defend the river valley against the Danes. The fort may have been surrounded by tidal waters at that date. The church is partly Norman in origin, perhaps earlier. Part of a Roman pavement was uncovered by grave-digging in the late 19th century.

Park at Parham Post (OS map ref. 070125) which can be reached along a 'No Through Road' which leaves the B2139 road about 1½ miles south-west of Storrington and climbs to the top of the Downs, where there is a large parking area.

From the car park cross over the South Downs Way and follow a broad track between fences which descends gently in a south-westerly direction, soon with an area of scrub on the right, and views ahead to the coastal plain. Where the scrubby area ends keep straight on with a fence on your left, still on a clear track. Immediately short of a copse ahead turn right and cross a short section of open field to a crossing track where turn left.

In 300 yards ignore two tracks to the right and continue ahead over the low summit of Wepham Down. In another 400 yards, just short of a double metal field gate, turn sharply back right following parallel to a gallop which curves left and climbs to the top of Perry Hill, where there are extensive views southwards over the coastal plain, westwards over the Arun Valley to Arundel Park and Castle and north-westwards to Bexley Hill and Blackdown on the Surrey border. A path dropping down the hill to the right (not used on the present walk) runs on the line of the so-called 'Lepers Path' which linked a leper settlement on the site of Angmering Lea Farm to the east with the chapel of St. James which stood near Offham in the Arun valley until the 15th century.

45

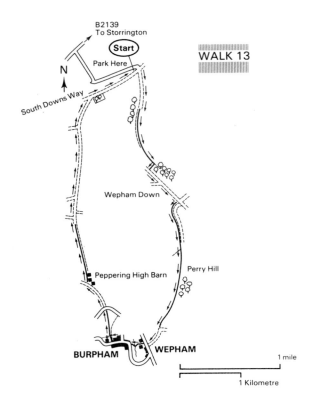

B2139
To Storrington

Start

Park Here

N

South Downs Way

WALK 13

Wepham Down

Peppering High Barn

Perry Hill

BURPHAM

WEPHAM

1 mile

1 Kilometre

When the path forks near the top of the hill, keep right and follow the shoulder of Perry Hill with the village of Burpham spread out below in the valley to the right. At a T-junction keep right and drop down to the road in the tiny hamlet of Wepham. Turn right along the road for 80 yards and then take a concrete track to the left. In 60 yards, keep to the right of a thatched barn and in a few more yards go right over a stile and round to the right of a second thatched barn. Now drop down across a field, go over a stile, and bear right down a flight of steps to a stream crossing and on to a road where you turn right and climb, ignoring a right turn, to reach the George and Dragon public house in the village of Burpham.

Go into the churchyard opposite the pub and keep round to the right of the church. Do not go through a gap in the wall on the right but climb three steps and go over a low section of wall ahead to follow a narrow path between fence and hedge. Where the enclosed section of the path ends bear diagonally left across the middle of the field

46

aiming a little to the right of the roofs of farm buildings which can just be seen over the low summit of the field. Go over a stile in the far right hand corner of the field to join a road. (A diversion of this path is proposed which would follow the field boundary straight ahead from the end of the enclosed section of path. If it is confirmed and signposted, please use it.)

Whichever route is followed, continue the walk northwards along the access track to the farm buildings at Peppering High Barn. Keep round to the left of the farm buildings and then fork right up a concrete track which continues to curve past the buildings and a silage pit and then becomes a dirt track, between fences at first and then with a fence to the right.

Now keep straight ahead for 3 miles, climbing gently and ignoring all paths to the right and left, finally reaching the South Downs Way at the top of the scarp slope just to the left of a clump of trees which can be seen on the skyline as you ascend. Turn right on the South Downs Way from which there are splendid views over the Weald. Tucked under the Downs can be seen the magnificent Elizabethan mansion of Parham, built in 1580 and carefully restored early in the present century. It is set in a 500 acre deer park and is open to the public on certain days during the summer months.

Follow the South Downs Way for a little over $\frac{1}{2}$ mile back to the car park.

Hammerpot and Patching Hill

Although longer than some in this book this is not a strenuous walk and passes through a mostly wooded stretch of the southern slope of the Downs where they begin to climb gently up from the coastal plain. It reaches a height of 468 feet on Barpham Hill, with views across miles of downland and also over the Arun valley to Arundel Park and Castle, only 3 miles away. The path through Patching Woods can be extremely muddy.

Patching is an attractive village of flint and thatch. The church is plain and bare, with a good timber roof and a handsome shingled spire.

This walk can be combined with Walk 15 to give a round trip of about 13½ miles. The linking route is included with the walk description and indicated on the sketch map.

Park on the redundant loop of the old A27 road at Hammerpot. This is now a cul-de-sac to the left (north) of the A27 Arundel–Worthing road, three miles east of Arundel, and forms the access road to the Woodmans Arms public house (OS map ref. 067057). There is a grass verge which provides adequate but not ample parking space.

Start the walk by going north on an enclosed grassy bridleway which leaves the cul-de-sac road immediately to the west of the Woodmans Arms car park. Follow this path for 100 yards only before turning right over two stiles and a plank bridge into a field. Now keep along the left hand edge of two fields to join a rough track just to the right of a flint barn.

Turn left along this track for less than 100 yards before going right on a rough track into woodland. After leaving the wooded area over two stiles, strike out diagonally to the right (north-east) aiming for some brick buildings which can just be seen through a line of trees. Cross this line of trees where the path is indicated by two stiles and continue diagonally, still north-east, across the next field. In the far left corner of this field, go over a stile and turn right for a few yards on a farm track to a T-junction.

Turn left at the T-junction, and in 150 yards, where woodland begins on the left of the path, turn right on a flinty track which leads through a metal field gate and along the right hand edge of two fields, then over a crossing track and along the right hand edge of a third

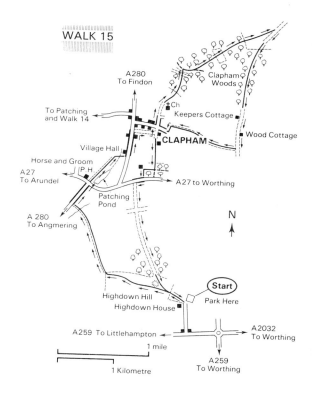

WALK 15

To Patching and Walk 14 ←

A280
To Findon

Clapham Woods

Ch
Keepers Cottage

■ Wood Cottage

CLAPHAM

Village Hall

Horse and Groom
A27
To Arundel
P.H.

A 280
To Angmering

Patching Pond

A27 to Worthing

N
↑

(Start)
Park Here

Highdown Hill
Highdown House ■

A259 To Littlehampton ←

A2032
To Worthing

1 mile

1 Kilometre

A259
To Worthing

a hedge and then a barbed wire fence on your left. At the bottom of the slope go over a footbridge and two more stiles and then skirt to the right of a fenced sewage area to join the main A280 road.

Turn right along this busy road for 350 yards to its junction with the even busier A27. Go straight across the A27 and take a grassy path to the right of the Horse and Groom public house and outbuildings, with Patching Pond on your right. Go over a stile and keep ahead with a hedge to the left and the pond a little way away to the right. On reaching a stile in the hedge on the left, *don't* go over it but instead bear away from the hedge diagonally to the right and slightly downhill to cross another stile and then climb in the same direction for 60 yards to a third stile giving access to a cricket ground. Cross the cricket ground and join a road immediately to the right of the village hall. Turn left along the road for about 160 yards and then, about 50 yards before reaching a right turn to Clapham village, turn right on a narrow metalled driveway lined on the right by a row of lime trees.

(To link with Walk 14 continue on up the main road for 200 yards before turning left on a narrow road, signposted Patching Street. Follow this for a little over $\frac{1}{4}$ mile and then turn right at a T-junction on the cul-de-sac to Patching church. Fork left along the rough track towards the church and in a few yards bear left through farm buildings. Immediately beyond the buildings bear round to the right on a flint track between fences. You are now on Walk 14.)

To continue with Walk 15 follow the driveway lined with lime trees which soon becomes a narrow path between fences and leads out to a track opposite a house called Summerfield. For the shorter walk of $3\frac{1}{2}$ miles turn right here and skip the next three paragraphs of description, but if you have time it is worth following the longer walk at least as far as the lovely little church of Clapham.

To follow the longer 6 mile walk, turn left at Summerfield and follow the track out to a road. Go straight across this road and ahead along another road, soon keeping straight on along a rough track between fences and over a crossing track to reach Clapham church. Go through the churchyard, keeping round to the left of the church and leaving the churchyard over a stile. Cross a short open field and go over another stile into Clapham Woods. On reaching a cleared area, go straight over an oblique crossing track and follow a grassy headland path which soon re-enters the woods. At a T-junction go right, gradually climbing, and at the next Y-junction, go left with the main track, ignoring a left fork after a few more yards. In another 200 yards, ignore a right fork, always keeping on the main track which now levels out with views glimpsed through woods to the left.

Go straight across another small open area, completely surrounded by woods, and continue on a clear woodland track, now with a fence and a steep slope dropping away to your left. After leaving the woods over a stile, go ahead on a grassy track between fields for about 150 yards before doubling back to the right on a clear trackway between fences to re-enter Clapham Woods. Now descend, ignoring all side and crossing tracks.

After leaving the woods, pass Keeper's Cottage (right) and about 200 yards after passing Wood Cottage (left), turn right on a narrow path which follows a fence line westwards, first to the north of the fence and then to the south of it. In $\frac{1}{2}$ mile the path leads you out to a T-junction with a rough track. Turn left and follow this track round to the right and into Clapham village. In about 200 yards you will be able to recognize and turn left along the track by which you came into the village.

(The description of the shorter walk resumes here.)

Follow this track southwards through a field gate and down the left hand edge of a field. After passing some farm buildings on the left, go straight ahead through two gates and uphill with a fence and a derelict brickfield to the right. Continue on a track through open woodland. Within sight and sound of the A27 ahead, turn right on a crossing track which skirts the perimeter of an industrial area. Look out for a narrow path to the left with a 'no cycling' notice at the start of it and follow it out to the A27.

Go straight across the main road and turn right along it, using the pavement on the opposite side. In 100 yards turn left on a wide track, partly metalled. Go straight over a crossing track, then across an open area before climbing through woodland on to Highdown Hill, all on a clear track. At a National Trust notice bear left across the shoulder of the hill and so back to the car park.

Walk 16   Cissbury Ring

6½ or 7½ miles (10.5 or 12 km)

OS sheet 198

Starting from the edge of the coastal plain, this walk climbs quickly into bare and lonely downland, the slopes a patchwork of intense cultivation. Although of a fair length, it is mostly very easy going, much of it on broad, well used tracks. At least two of these are probably ancient, since they are among the half dozen rights of way which radiate from Cissbury.

Cissbury Ring, the largest and most spectacular prehistoric camp on the South Downs, was known simply as Bury until the 16th century (from the Old English *burh*, a stronghold). Although time has rounded the steep ramparts and partly filled in the ditches, it remains an impressive place. It has been calculated that 60,000 tons of chalk were moved in its making, and it has a long history. Originally a Neolithic camp, it was the scene of extensive flint mining, of which the only traces today are a number of depressions in the ground at the south-west end. Carbon dating of antler picks found in the excavated mine shafts suggest that this was about 2700 BC. Two Neolithic skeletons were also found. Later it became an important Iron Age fort, probably containing a sizeable community. It was farmed during the Roman period and then refortified against Saxon raiders. Looking north-east from Cissbury it is possible to detect the faint shadows of lynchets lying across some of the cornfields, a relic of very ancient cultivation, probably connected with Cissbury.

It is interesting to note that the track which the walk takes eastwards from Cissbury is an example of what is officially designated as a 'Road used as a Public Path'. This label is often a hint of antiquity and this particular road can be traced on the map running directly both westwards to the Arun and eastwards to the Adur at Coombes, where it could have linked with the Ridgeway at Botolphs. It is tempting to speculate that this might have been the track used for exporting the flints from the Cissbury mines to other parts of southern England.

Sompting church is famous for its tall and slender Saxon tower, with a strange gabled cap of a kind familiar in the Rhineland but unique in this country. The interior contains a rare example of Saxon sculpture.

This walk can be linked with Walk 19 to give a combined circuit of 12½ miles. The link is indicated in the route description.

Park at Sompting church (OS map ref. 162055). To get there turn right (north) off the A27 Brighton–Worthing road on to the unclassified road to Steyning which leaves the main road about a mile

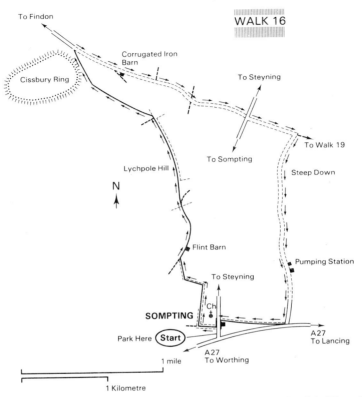

To Findon

Corrugated Iron Barn

Cissbury Ring

To Steyning

To Walk 19

To Sompting

Steep Down

Lychpole Hill

N

Flint Barn

Pumping Station

To Steyning

Ch

SOMPTING

Park Here (Start)

A27
To Lancing

A27
To Worthing

1 mile

1 Kilometre

west of Lancing and which is signposted to Sompting Parish Church. Park on the left of the road where it is at its widest, about 100 to 150 yards north of the junction with the A27.

Take a path to the left (westwards) off the Sompting–Steyning road, which leaves the road about 100 yards south of the church, opposite the entrance to the vicarage. Follow this narrow path for 200 yards and, just before reaching some allotments on the left of the path, turn right on another narrow path between fence and hedge which climbs on to the Downs. This soon becomes a wider track up the right hand edge of a field with a fence to the right. In 300 yards turn left along the top edge of this field still with a fence to the right. Ahead and slightly left you can see Highdown Hill which is the start and finish of Walk 15.

At the end of the field go right, now once again between fence and hedge. After passing through a bridle gate, keep straight on along a wide track with a belt of woodland on your left, soon keeping right with a more substantial track. Immediately after passing a flint barn on the right, keep left on the higher of two approximately parallel trackways round the base of Lychpole Hill. In a little over 400 yards, go through the leftmost of two field gates and immediately turn left at a Y-junction and climb on a clear track through scrub. This soon opens out on to an area of rough pasture and your route follows a well ridden track along the side of the hill eventually with a fence to the right and the scrub-covered side of Lychpole Hill up to the left.

In nearly a mile, after passing through a weighted bridle gate, ignore the first clear track going sharply back to the left and continue ahead for about 50 yards before forking left uphill through fairly dense scrub. Towards the top of the hill the path bisects a fairly narrow strip of open field where the route may not be well defined. Go straight across this cultivated strip and immediately on the other side, bear right on a crossing track which drops slightly downhill through scrub again with the hill dropping away to the right and the ramparts of Cissbury Ring away through the scrub to the left. Follow this track for about $\frac{1}{4}$ mile to the Cissbury Ring parking area.

From this point I can strongly recommend the walker to climb the clear track up on to Cissbury and to make a circuit of the outer ramparts, adding a mile to the total distance.

To continue with the rest of the walk, return to the car parking area and leave it by a clear chalk and flint track which doubles back to the right from the track by which you reached the car park before climbing on to Cissbury. Drop down into a valley in an easterly direction with a fence on your left and walking on a lower level than and roughly parallel to the track by which you approached Cissbury. In $\frac{1}{4}$ mile keep left by a corrugated iron barn, straight on along the lower of two tracks.

Follow the main track now for about $1\frac{1}{2}$ miles, ignoring side and cross tracks and going straight across the Sompting–Steyning road. About $\frac{1}{4}$ mile beyond the road turn right on a fenced track which follows a line of electricity pylons southwards along the western flank of Steep Down.

(To link with Walk 19 keep straight on instead of turning right and in a little more than 100 yards, turn right and climb on to Steep Down as described in Walk 19.)

Follow the track and the pylons southwards for $1\frac{1}{2}$ miles, passing a water pumping station and some derelict farm buildings on the left, to reach the main A27 dual carriageway. Turn right and follow the path on the near (north) side of the main road. In just over 100 yards, bear right on a grassy path with a hedge on your right. In about 50 yards go through a swing gate and follow the right hand edge of a field, diverging gradually from the A27, with woodland on your right. (The path winding into the woodland just before the swing gate is not a right of way.) In the far right hand corner of the field, go through a gate which brings you out on the road within yards of the start of the walk.

Walk 17   Chanctonbury Ring and Washington

$4\frac{1}{2}$ miles (7 km)

OS sheet 198

The main feature of this relatively short walk is Chanctonbury Ring, which must surely be the most famous landmark on the South Downs. The gentle climb up to the Ring follows one of the most attractive bostal (see p. 76) routes on the northern escarpment. After a fine stretch of the South Downs Way and a descent to the village of Washington, the circuit is completed through fields at the foot of the Downs and along the bottom of a hanger which covers the northern slope of the Downs below Chanctonbury Ring.

Chanctonbury Ring is the site of an Iron Age hill fort of which the rampart is just visible. Inside it were found the remains of a Romano-Celtic temple. Quite a few legends have become attached to it concerning encounters with the Devil at midnight on Midsummer's Eve and so forth, but more interesting is the clump of beech trees which has made it such a striking and immediately recognizable landmark. They were planted by Charles Goring of Wiston in 1760, when he was a schoolboy, and lovingly tended and watered by him with the 'almost hopeless wish' that he would see them properly established. He lived to 85 and his wish was granted. The sight of the clump, epitome of the Downs for so many, must have given pleasure to many thousands of lovers of Sussex ever since. Sadly, the trees do not look as happy as they used to, but strenuous replanting efforts are in hand. The hill is 800 feet up and offers views of almost the whole of Sussex, as well as a stretch of the Surrey hills and glimpses of Kent and Hampshire.

Washington stands at the northern end of an ancient river valley through the Downs from which the river vanished millions of years ago, leaving the so-called 'wind-gap' used by the A24 road.

Park at the car park and picnic area at the foot of Chanctonbury Hill. To reach it, turn left (south) off the A283 Steyning–Storrington road on to a narrow unclassified road (signposted to Chanctonbury) at OS map ref. 144135, about $2\frac{1}{2}$ miles north-west of Steyning. The car park and picnic area are on the left in about $\frac{3}{4}$ mile, almost at the foot of the Downs (OS map ref. 146124).

Continue southwards along the road by which you arrived. This soon becomes a rough chalk and flint track and you should follow this as it keeps to the right of an old quarry and then curves to the left above it. There are various unofficial short cuts straight up the wooded slope to

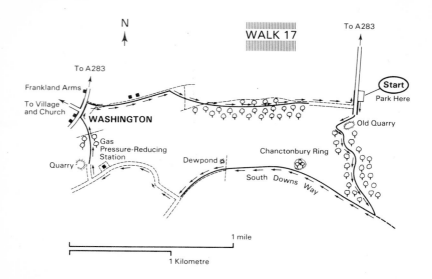

N

WALK 17

To A283

To A283

Frankland Arms

To Village
and Church

WASHINGTON

Start

Park Here

Old Quarry

Gas
Pressure-Reducing
Station

Quarry

Dewpond

Chanctonbury Ring

South Downs Way

1 mile

1 Kilometre

Chanctonbury Ring, but the right of way follows the main track on a more gentle ascent through woodland and out on to the open downland at the top. On reaching the wide South Downs Way crossing track, turn right and follow it up to Chanctonbury Ring.

Continue westwards with the South Downs Way. In about 600 yards, just beyond a crossing fence line, look out for a dewpond on the right of the track. Dewponds, which are such a feature of the Downs, are, in spite of their picturesque name, shallow depressions lined with clay (or sometimes concrete nowadays) which collect rainwater rather than dew. Before the days of piped water supplies they were a vital source of water for the huge flocks of sheep which used to crop the dry chalk downland. Nowadays they are often leaky, dry and grass-grown. This example, one of the highest on the Downs, was restored by the Society of Sussex Downsmen in 1971.

Keep on along the South Downs Way from which there are good views of Cissbury Ring (Walk 16) away to the south. About ¼ mile beyond the dewpond, turn right, still with the South Downs Way, and follow it downhill passing a gas pressure-reducing station on the right. This unattractive intrusion into the downland achieves the unique distinction of polluting the landscape by sight, sound *and* smell. Astonishingly, it could be and was established without being subject to any kind of planning control. Hurry past it, and in about 200 yards, turn right off the South Downs Way on a clear chalky track which, after about 150 yards, becomes a rather narrow overgrown path which drops down with a chalk quarry to the left. Descend through woodland and over a stile, finally crossing an open field to a road.

60

The White Horse, Chilgrove (Walk 4)

The church and village well at East Marden (Walk 5)

Stane Street south of Bignor Post (Walk 9)

Poynings village with Newtimber Hill beyond (Walks 20 and 21)

Chanctonbury Ring and the western Downs (Walk 21)

Alfriston church and the River Cuckmere (Walk 27)

Walk 19

5 miles (8 km)

OS sheet 198

<h1 style="text-align:right">Coombes and Steep Down</h1>

This is a fairly easy but exhilarating walk, up and down across open cultivated downland to the west of the Adur valley. It offers a succession of magnificent views and goes through the interesting hamlet of Coombes. The path drops down into Coombes through a wood on the side of a combe which probably gave it its name. All that remains of the village are a few houses and a farm clustered round a tiny Saxon church of grey knapped flints, with a roof of Horsham stone and a little red-tiled belfry. It is primitive, unrestored, atmospheric and endearing. The chancel arch is no more than a simple rounded doorway. The faded and rather fragmentary wall paintings were discovered in 1949 and are thought to be pre-12th century. There are signs that a bank originally enclosed the churchyard, suggesting that the church was built on a pre-Christian religious site.

A link with Walk 16 is indicated in the route description, a combined circuit of $12\frac{1}{2}$ miles.

Park on the edge of the Downs to the north of North Lancing. The car parking area can be reached by turning right (north), signposted North Lancing, at the roundabout on the A27 Shoreham–Worthing road about 2 miles west of the River Adur (OS map ref. 186055). In 300 yards turn right into Mill Road and climb to the Downs, finally forking left on a rough track. The car park is to the left of this track in about 100 yards (OS map ref. 184062).

Start the walk by going over the track by which you approached the Downs. Cross a rough grassy area to follow a track which skirts an old quarry area. In a few yards only, turn left over a stile and go straight across the first field, aiming for another stile. Follow a clear track across the next field over a low summit, soon aiming for the chimney of Shoreham cement works which can be seen across the Adur valley. Go over another stile and drop down into a valley on a path between fences. At the bottom, pass to the right of a flint-walled enclosure and climb again, soon with a line of trees to your right. Beyond the trees, where the track curves to the right through a metal gate, keep straight ahead over a stile, then across a concrete track and over another stile. Keep up along the right hand edge of the next field with a line of trees once again on your right as you go over a summit. Ignore a track which goes back to the right and keep ahead, now with a fence line to your right. Go over another stile and keep along the left hand edge of

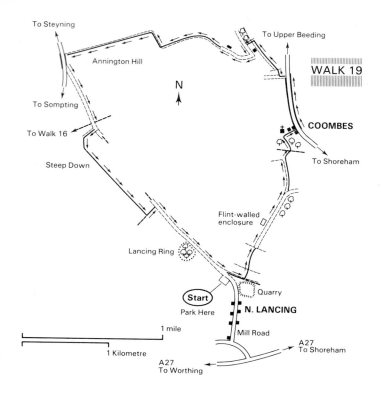

the next field as you go over another summit. In about 200 yards, where the fence line turns away to the left, go slightly right across an open field aiming a little to the left of the cement works chimney. Drop down on a narrow path through woodland to the beautiful downland church of Coombes.

After leaving the churchyard, descend across a paddock and out on to a farm track which leads you out through the handful of houses which make up the hamlet of Coombes to a road.

Turn left along the road for about ¼ mile. Although unclassified it can be rather busy at weekends, but there is a reasonable verge for most of the distance. A few yards before the road passes under power lines, turn left through a metal gate on a dirt track, almost immediately forking right on the lower of two tracks. In 10 yards turn right through a metal gate and drop down a steep grassy bank and through an area of scrub. At the bottom, go through a bridle gate and across the corner of a field and through another metal gate. Now keep along the left hand edge of a field for ⅓ mile with a hedge on your left.

66

Follow this hedge line through field gates and past a white-walled cottage on the left. About 150 yards after passing the cottage turn left through a bridle gate and climb through a narrow strip of woodland to a T-junction with a broad track. Turn left along this track and follow it round to the right past the entrance to the cottage called Tinpots.

The odd name of the cottage has been linked with the fact that this was the ancient route by which tin was conveyed from Cornwall to the seaport of Pevensey. There may have been a Roman bridge across the river nearby.

About 120 yards after you have curved to the right by Tinpots, now on the South Downs Way, go through a metal gate and bear right with the main track. After passing a silage pit on the right, go through another gate and climb along the shoulder of Annington Hill with a fence on your left. From this path there are views of Bramber with its prominent castle ruin, away to the right. Beyond another field gate, the South Downs Way has (so far unofficially) been diverted down the hill to the right and round the right hand edge of a large field. Follow the edge of the field round and up to the Steyning–Sompting road on the top of the hill.

Turn left along the road for 100 yards only before forking left on a clear track. Follow this for $\frac{1}{2}$ mile to the foot of Steep Down where you go over a crossing track, under power lines and through a metal gate before turning right and climbing fairly steeply with a fence on your right to the triangulation point on the top of Steep Down. (To link with Walk 16, turn right on the crossing track at the foot of Steep Down.)

From the summit there are extensive views in all directions. All round to the north there is a great expanse of bare rolling downland and a segment of the Weald beyond. To the south-east there are views across the Adur, where it widens on its approach to Shoreham harbour, to the distant chalk cliffs beyond Brighton. To the south-west, beyond the coastal plain, you might catch a glimpse of the Isle of Wight and westwards, not far away, the crest of Cissbury (Walk 16) is visible.

From the triangulation point bear left along the ridge of Steep Down, heading south-east towards the clump of trees on the next hill, known as Lancing Ring. At the bottom of the hill, at a T-junction, turn left and in a little more than 50 yards turn sharply right. Climb on a clear track which passes to the left of Lancing Ring and descends, taking you straight back to the car park.

This walk begins by turning away from the Downs and following some less well trodden paths across Wealden farmland. After a sharp climb to the hills from Poynings it skirts the rim of the Devil's Dyke, the most striking combe on the South Downs. The rest is easy going along the ridgeway with a final descent to the Shepherd and Dog at Fulking where the walk begins and ends.

Fulking, a village rather unusually without a church, is situated at the foot of one of the most dramatic escarpments in the entire length of the Downs. It is also the most characteristic of all the downland spring-line villages. The spring, which never fails (it kept going even during the catastrophic drought of 1976), gushes out of the steep hillside in a copse just above the Shepherd and Dog and runs down to the roadside. Esther Meynell, in her book on Sussex published in 1947, relates that in the old days of sheep-rearing on the Downs the stream used to be dammed in this hollow and a sheepwash made in the bend of the lane. The pub probably gets its name from this.

Poynings, another spring-line village tucked against the foot of the scarp slope, has a very fine cruciform church with a massive, battlemented square tower. The interior is beautifully light and lofty. It has often been compared with the church at Alfriston (Walk 27).

The Devil's Dyke has always been popular. In the Railway Age it was thought worth building a branch line from the coast to bring tourists almost to the top of the hill. The railway has gone but the Dyke still attracts thousands of visitors, though most of them do not usually stray far from the car park. This walk keeps just far enough away from the cars to avoid most of the crowds.

Park at Fulking which is situated on the unclassified road running along the foot of the Downs linking the A281 Pyecombe–Henfield road with the A2037 Upper Beeding–Henfield road. It is possible to park at several places on the roadside verge immediately to the west of the village. The ideal spot, if there is room, is immediately west of the Shepherd and Dog public house, near a roadside stream (OS map ref. 246113).

Start off by walking back into the village from the Shepherd and Dog. In a little over 100 yards, about 50 yards before reaching a shop on the left, turn left on a metalled access track which takes you into a recreation ground. Keep along the right hand edge of this open grassy area,

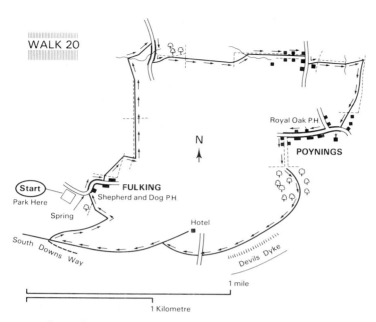

WALK 20

N
↑

Royal Oak P.H

POYNINGS

Start
Park Here

FULKING
Shepherd and Dog P.H

Spring

Hotel

South Downs Way

Devils Dyke

1 mile

1 Kilometre

over wooden railings and then diagonally right across an open field (if it is under cultivation it may be best to keep round the right hand edge). At the far right hand corner of this field go through a gap over a culvert and keep along the right hand edge of the next field, now in an easterly direction. At the first field corner go ahead over a stile and immediately turn left nd follow the left hand edge of a field, now heading north. Follow the hedland northwards for $\frac{1}{4}$ mile on a stiled path, finally keeping to the left of a Nissen hut. Keep along the left hand edge of a paddock and, where the hedge veers away to the left, go ahead to find and cross a stile and a plank bridge over a stream. Immediately beyond the stream, turn right and after crossing two more narrow stiles, bear slightly left across a meadow and through a field gate. Keep straight on with the stream to your right and go through a rather damp and overgrown area to reach a road.

Turn right along the road for about 250 yards, and then go left through a rather dilapidated bridle gate converted into a stile beside a metal field gate. Go slightly left and uphill to the corner of a copse and then follow the left hand edge of the field with woodland to the left, now in an easterly direction and parallel to the Downs. Keep going east over an open field, passing under power lines and following the top of a low ridge. Newtimber Hill, with its wooded summit, is directly ahead. In the next field, bear slightly left and down hill, and after crossing the corner of a third field, go over a footbridge by a clump of trees. Continue eastwards over a stile and on between hedge and stream. After passing to the left of a flint barn, follow a more substantial track out to a road.

Turn right along the road for 60 yards and then go left on a metalled track through a school playground, passing to the left of a school hall. Go over a stile and continue along the left hand edge of a field. In the next field corner, cross a stile and stream and head across the next field aiming for a field gate with Newtimber Hill still directly ahead. Do not go through the field gate but turn right just short of it and follow the left hand edge of a field with a fence and low bank to the left, aiming now for some farm buildings which can be seen ahead, a little to the left of Poynings church. On approaching the farm, veer slightly right, away from the fence line, and head towards a Dutch barn with the church beyond. Go through the farmyard and out to a road opposite the church.

Turn right along the road, and in 50 yards, at a T-junction, turn left. Now, to avoid walking on the road, take a parallel path which starts through a stone archway on the right of the road. About 100 yards after passing the Royal Oak public house on the right, and almost opposite the entrance to Dyke Farm House, turn left on a metalled driveway which soon becomes a rough track between fence and hedge. At the foot of the steep wooded slope of the Downs, where the path divides into three, take the left hand track and follow it up through woodland and out on to scrub-covered hillside. As the path levels out it follows the edge of the Devil's Dyke which drops steeply away to the left. Ignore cross tracks and follow the main track out to a road.

Keep straight ahead across the road and over a stile to follow a path along a line of earthworks and past a triangulation point to reach the edge of the northern escarpment with a tremendous view over the Weald. Turn left and follow the edge of the escarpment. After passing through a bridle gate keep left and slightly uphill. In about $\frac{1}{2}$ mile, where the main chalky South Downs Way converges from the left in a slight dip, double back sharply to the right, downhill, on a track hollowed out quite deeply between banks. About halfway down the hill, double back sharply to the left on a crossing track and follow it downhill, through a belt of scrub and then along the left hand edge of a field towards the buildings of Fulking village. About two-thirds of the way along the field, go left over a stile and descend through the car park of the Shepherd and Dog public house and so back to the start of the walk.

Wolstonbury and Newtimber

You will have to contend with several ups and downs on this walk but the ups are in each case a good deal less steep than the downs. You will encounter scarp, beech woods, open grassy hilltops, chalk pits, tiny churches, Iron Age ramparts and immense views of Downs and Weald – the downland in microcosm and a splendid introduction to this unique landscape.

Wolstonbury Hill, 670 feet high, stands clear of the line of the Downs and is a landmark for miles. Its crest is encircled by the ramparts of an Iron Age fort. The views are superb – Ashdown Forest to the north-east, the Surrey Hills and Blackdown to the north-west.

The Devil's Dyke, seen from afar and to good effect from Newtimber Hill on this walk, is a steep-sided combe eroded in the escarpment. Some geologists think it might have been excavated during the Ice Age by water flowing from a thawing ice cap, but, if so, the debris has inexplicably vanished. An earlier theory ascribes it to the Devil, who, annoyed by the number of churches in the Weald, tried one night to cut a dyke through the Downs to let in the sea and drown the Christians. Mistaking an old woman's candle at a cottage window for the dawn, he hurriedly abandoned the task.

The church at Newtimber is mostly a Victorian restoration, but attractively set in the valley between the hills of Wolstonbury and Newtimber, among the trees and the few houses which are all that survive of the village. These include Newtimber Place, a moated 17th century manor which is occasionally open to the public. 238 acres of Newtimber Hill are owned by the National Trust who have cut a number of paths through the woods on the northern slope, one of which is used on this walk.

Pyecombe is a scattered village on the A23. It has a little flint church, partly Norman, with an unusual lead font, 12th century and beautifully ornamented. The village was famous years ago for the making of shepherds' crooks.

Park at New Way Lane under Wolstonbury Hill. New Way Lane is a turning westwards off the A273 Pyecombe–Burgess Hill road at Clayton, immediately to the south of the Jack and Jill public house at OS map ref. 299142. Follow the lane westwards for about ¾ mile and park on the grass verge a few yards after the lane turns north at OS map ref. 289143.

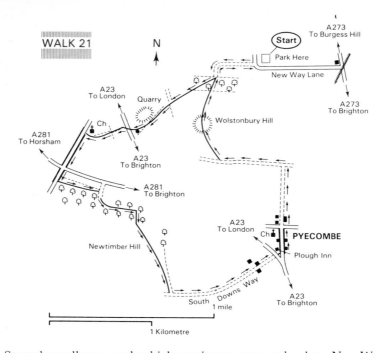

Start the walk on a path which continues westwards where New Way
Lane turns sharply north. In about 250 yards turn left (south) with a
clear track and enter the beechwoods at the foot of Wolstonbury Hill.
Almost immediately after entering the woods, go over a crossing track
and a stile and, in a few more yards, bear right on a track which climbs
diagonally up the hill. In a few more yards ignore a narrow track
which breaks away to the left and climbs steeply up the hill and
instead keep ahead on the main track which ascends more gently.
After climbing out of the woodland, follow this fine terraced path up
round the shoulder of the hill, with views ahead to Chanctonbury
Ring and the western Downs. After crossing a rough stile in a fence
line the path is less well defined but you should continue ahead along
the grassy hillside with old quarry workings away up the hill to the
left. Aim towards the wooded slopes of Newtimber Hill which can be
seen ahead across the valley. After passing through an area of
scattered scrub, go through a weighted bridle gate and immediately
turn left on a crossing track for 5 yards only before turning right over a
stile. Now drop steeply downhill with a barbed wire fence to your
right, aiming just to the left of more modern quarry workings in the
valley. The path is not very obvious but you should skirt closely to the
left of the quarry with the steep hillside rising on the left. Immediately
beyond the quarry, go over a stile in the fence line to the right and
follow a clear chalky track past some buildings and out to the main
A23 dual carriageway.

72

Turn right along the main road for about 50 yards and then cross it where there is a gap in the central reservation wall. Take a narrow path almost opposite which starts between metal railings. In a few yards go ahead through a wooden field gate and along the left hand edge of a field. At the corner of this field go over a stile and keep along the right hand edge of the next field to Newtimber church. Go over a stile into the churchyard, follow the main church path out to a road and turn left.

Follow this road for a little over $\frac{1}{4}$ mile and then go straight across the main A281 Brighton–Horsham road into Beggars Lane, passing a National Trust notice 'Newtimber Hill' on the right. In about 200 yards take a National Trust footpath to the left which climbs up some steps on to the side of Newtimber Hill. In about 150 yards, where the path forks, take the lower left hand path which traverses the wooded hillside, climbing gently at first and then descending to a T-junction with a bridleway where you should turn right.

Follow this clear track which curves to the left and climbs to the top of Newtimber Hill. Ignore side tracks, and after passing through a bridle gate near the top, keep straight ahead up pasture and out on to the open grassy summit continuing over grassed area (there is no defined path) is a south-easterly direction, walking approximately parallel to a thin line of trees some distance away to the left, beyond which can be seen the twin windmills known as Jack and Jill. Converge gradually on the hedge line to the left of the open area. As you cross the summit there are good views of the deep rift of the Devil's Dyke across the valley to the right.

Follow the hedge line to the far left corner of the open grassy National Trust area and here turn left through two bridle gates and follow the left hand edge of a field in an easterly direction, now on the South Downs Way. In $\frac{1}{4}$ mile, bear left and drop down on a wide chalky track to the A23 at Pyecombe.

Cross the main road and keep to the right of the Plough Inn to follow the narrow Pyecombe village street up to the church. Pass the church on your left and on reaching a T-junction of roads, go straight ahead on a rough track which passes some houses and then narrows. Follow this path for $\frac{1}{2}$ mile to a wide crossing track where you should turn left through a bridle gate to the right of a field gate. After a further $\frac{1}{2}$ mile and about 150 yards after passing through a field gate, turn right on a green strip across an open field, aiming for the summit of Wolstonbury Hill. After crossing a stile climb to the triangulation point on the top.

From here, drop down the steep north slope of the hill, aiming towards the farm and mansion of the Danny estate in the valley below. The path is not very well defined at first as it winds through the Iron Age earthworks but is much clearer on the steep slope. Towards the bottom of the hill go through a belt of woodland to rejoin your outgoing route and retrace your footsteps to the car parking area.

Walk 22 Ditchling Beacon and East Chiltington

6½ miles (10.5 km)

OS sheet 198

Ditchling Beacon, at 813 feet, is one of the three highest points on the South Downs, with magnificent views across the Weald towards Blackdown in the west, Ashdown Forest to the north-east, and in between them the Surrey hills and, on a clear day, the white chalk pits of the North Downs.

The walk, starting high up on the chalk, drops quickly into the Weald and follows a sandy ridge eastwards from Streat, with fine views of the long bare skyline of the Downs, before climbing up on to the chalk again via Plumpton Bostal. During the last 1½ miles along the ancient ridgeway followed by the South Downs Way, it is interesting to look down on the Weald and pick out the route of the first part of the walk, clearly marked by the little churches at Westmeston, Streat, East Chiltington and Plumpton.

Park in the car park at the top of Ditchling Beacon (OS map ref. 333130). This can be reached by taking the Ditchling road north out of Brighton, crossing the ring road at Old Boat corner (OS map ref. 325095) and continuing northwards to the top of the Downs. Alternatively you can take the steep and winding road which climbs to the top of the beacon from Ditchling village.

Cross the road from the car park and start off eastwards along the South Downs Way. In a few yards only, however, drop down to the left over a double stile and obliquely down the escarpment on a clear path. In an area of old quarry workings near the bottom of the hill, turn left on a wider track and follow it down through a gate and on within a line of trees and past farm buildings to the road at Westmeston.

Westmeston is one of many spring-line villages dotted along the foot of the northern scarp of the Downs where water rises out of the base of the chalk. It has a characteristic downland church which has been much restored but still has its 14th century timber porch.

Turn right along the main road, passing the church on your left (there is a wide grass verge), and a little over 100 yards beyond the church go left over a stile by a field gate and half right across a field, looking out for another stile which takes you into an enclosed track between hedge and metal fence. This leads out to a broad gravel track where you should turn left. Now follow this clear track northwards for almost a mile. On reaching the buildings of Hayleigh Farm turn right

74

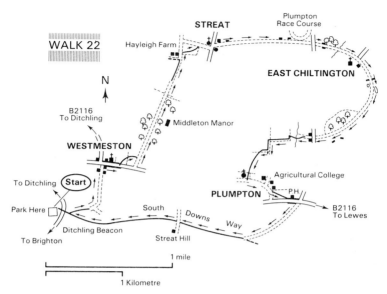

STREAT

Plumpton
Race Course

Hayleigh Farm

EAST CHILTINGTON

N

B2116
To Ditchling

Middleton Manor

WESTMESTON

Agricultural College

To Ditchling (Start)

PLUMPTON

P.H

Park Here

B2116
To Lewes

South

Downs

Way

Ditchling Beacon

Streat Hill

To Brighton

1 mile

1 Kilometre

between some fuel storage tanks to find steps and a stile. Beyond the
stile the line of the path is diagonally half left uphill across the open
field, but if the field is under cultivation it might be best to follow the
fence line straight ahead and turn left on the near side of the first
hedge line. In the top corner of the field join a broad track at a gate.

At this point and at various stages during the next $1\frac{1}{2}$ miles there are
fine views across to the Downs. The 'V' of trees visible on the scarp slope
was planted in commemoration of Queen Victoria's jubilee in 1887.

Turn right along the track and follow it past Streat church to a road
where turn left. Streat is beautifully situated on a sandy ridge running
east to west. The name derives from the Roman road which followed
this ridge on its way to join Stane Street in the Arun valley (see Walk
9).

Having turned left, follow the road for 60 yards and then, opposite a
letter-box in a brick pillar, turn right on a wide track. Continue
eastwards on this track for nearly a mile, finally on a metalled section
along the southern perimeter of Plumpton Race Course. This part is
actually on the line of the Roman road. Just beyond the race course go
straight across a road and continue almost straight ahead, still on a
wide track, for about $\frac{1}{2}$ mile to the small 12th to 14th century church of
East Chiltington.

Immediately after passing the church, turn right following the
churchyard wall round and in a few yards bear away left, following
the main track through a gateway signposted 'Footpath Only

Plumpton Lane'. Follow this roughly metalled track for nearly a mile out to a road.

Go straight across the road and take a narrow path between hedges which starts immediately to the right of a letter-box. In a few yards go over a stile and drop down diagonally left across a field to a stream which is crossed by stepping stones. Go half right across the next field passing just to the left of a cattle shelter and go through a bridle gate in the corner and then over a rail. Keep round the left hand edge of two sides of the next field and after going through a field gate in the far left corner turn left on a dirt track. In 170 yards (under overhead wires) turn right along the near side of a hedge and ditch and in a few yards go left over a sleeper bridge. Now strike out across the next field aiming directly towards Plumpton church – there is no visible path. Go over a stile by some meteorological instruments and keep straight ahead on a green strip to cross another stile into the corner of Plumpton churchyard. Plumpton church with its attractive shingled spire is mainly 13th century.

Leave the churchyard through the main entrance and turn left on a path between hedge and wooden fence, passing the buildings of Plumpton Agricultural College. On reaching the college access road turn right and in about 100 yards, where the road curves right, go left through a bridle gate. In less than 10 yards go right over wooden railings and go diagonally left aiming for the far right hand corner of a large paddock where you join the B2116 road at the Half Moon public house.

Turn left at the road and in 100 yards, opposite a road turning to Plumpton Green, turn right on a roughly metalled track, Plumpton Bostal. 'Bostal' is a Sussex dialect word for the steep paths climbing the escarpment of the South Downs. Often sunken or terraced, these tracks are usually very old, sometimes Roman, more often earlier.

Follow the bostal to the top of the Downs. On reaching the summit, turn right on the South Downs Way and follow it for $1\frac{1}{2}$ miles back to the car park.

Walk 23

Woodingdean and Iford Hill

6 miles (9.5 km)

OS sheet 198

Although starting from the outskirts of Brighton, this is a walk which, for much of its length, crosses bare and surprisingly remote downland, following clear tracks through arable land and also traversing open stretches of grassland. There is a steady climb from Balsdean valley up on to the high ridge, rewarded by fine views across the Ouse Valley towards Lewes, the Weald beyond, and the dip in the land between the headlands of Mount Caburn and Firle Beacon. The Ouse Valley was at one time an estuary and sea-going ships sailed as far inland as Lewes, passing Rodmell and Iford, villages visible near the foot of the hill.

The last lap of the walk overlooks the long dry valley between Lewes and Brighton, with glimpses of Falmer church, and further away the spire of Stanmer church in the park which it now shares with Sussex University, part of which is also visible.

Park on the B2133 Falmer to Rottingdean road to the north of Woodingdean. There is space to park off the road about 100 yards north of the Acres bakery on the northern outskirts of Woodingdean at OS map ref. 356064.

From the car parking area start the walk eastwards from the road, immediately forking right to follow a track which runs parallel to and a little distance away from the built-up area of Woodingdean to the right. In $\frac{1}{3}$ mile keep right at a fork and pass to the right of a radio mast. In $\frac{1}{4}$ mile go over a crossing track and follow a path which runs close to some houses and gardens and then bears away from the houses slightly downhill. After going through a bridle gate keep to the right hand edge of the field ahead with a barbed wire fence to your right, climbing gently and soon aiming for a grassy reservoir mound which comes into sight ahead. After passing through another bridle gate and under power lines, bear slightly left, away from the fence line on your right to join a metalled access road at a bridle gate. Turn sharply left along the road and descend into a valley.

At the bottom where the road doubles back to the right at a 'Private Road' notice, keep left through a metal gate, and, in 50 yards, where the main track curves to the left along the floor of the valley, go ahead through a bridle gate and follow a clear track which can be seen climbing up the hill out of the valley.

At the point where the path levels out, turn left through a gate by a

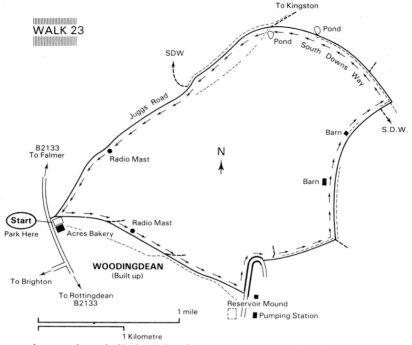

To Kingston

SDW

Pond

Pond

South Downs Way

Juggs Road

B2133
To Falmer

Radio Mast

N

Barn

S.D.W.

Barn

Start

Park Here

Radio Mast

Acres Bakery

To Brighton

WOODINGDEAN
(Built up)

To Rottingdean
B2133

Reservoir Mound

Pumping Station

1 mile

1 Kilometre

cattle trough and climb with a fence on your right, heading a little to the right of a barn, the roof of which can be seen on the skyline. After passing this barn, keep straight ahead over open downland. After passing to the right of another barn the track soon acquires a concrete surface and takes you to the edge of the escarpment. Where the concrete track turns away to the right, go ahead on a grassy path and in about 50 yards go through a swing gate and turn left, following a barbed wire fence on your left. Follow this superb ridge path (part of the South Downs Way) along the edge of the Downs above the village of Kingston for about a mile.

Soon after passing a pond on your right, bear left between gate posts, passing another pond on the left, and follow a clear track. This is Jugg's Road, the old route between Brighton and Lewes over the Downs and was used by the Brighton fishwives to bring their husbands' catch for sale in Lewes. It was originally known as 'Juggs Bostal' and was called after the nickname 'Jug' given to the Brighton fishermen.

Where the track opens out on to a wide grassy slope, the official route follows the fence on the right, though most walkers seem to use the higher path to the left. After passing through a metal field gate the South Downs Way forks to the right, but you should keep straight on along a roughly metalled track which takes you up over Newmarket Hill, past a radio mast, and back to the car park.

Mount Caburn is a promontory at the southernmost point of a small outlier of the South Downs which is cut off from the rest of the hills by a ring of marshland and the River Ouse flowing at the foot of its cliff-like western escarpment. The walk crosses and recrosses the outlier, opening up a succession of views of the surrounding countryside – marsh, downland and Weald as well as the county town of Lewes.

For some of its length the walk is not on rights of way but follows paths licensed for public use by the Glynde Estate. Please be particularly careful to keep to the described route. The outgoing path from Caburn to the hill above Lewes (which *is* a right of way) is not easily usable on its correct line because of obstructions. I have therefore described the nearest practicable route which does not interfere with agriculture and is already well used. There are problems, too, with the footpath across Lewes Golf Course and I have suggested a modification which avoids crossing too much of the playing area.

Glynde is a neat and attractive village curving round the foot of Mount Caburn. For centuries it was part of the estate of Glynde Place, an Elizabethan house which is sometimes open to the public. The church, unlike most downland churches, was built in the Palladian style for the estate in 1763.

Park at Glynde. If approaching from Lewes, fork left off the A27 Lewes to Eastbourne road into Ranscombe Lane about ½ mile east of the eastern end of the Lewes bypass. On reaching a T-junction in the village, turn left and you can park almost anywhere along the wide village street. There is a particularly convenient area off the road to the right under some trees about 100 yards beyond the church and the entrance to Glynde Place (OS map ref. 456094).

Start the walk by returning down the village street and turning right into Ranscombe Lane. About 20 yards after passing the post office on the left, turn right over a stile. Go straight across the first field to another stile and then follow a well trodden path across the next field to cross a stile to the left of some trees. Go ahead up over the shoulder of the hill. At a crossing track, turn left and climb to the top of Mount Caburn.

Mount Caburn hill-fort dominates the river valley, which was an estuary until the Middle Ages. It had a long history of over five

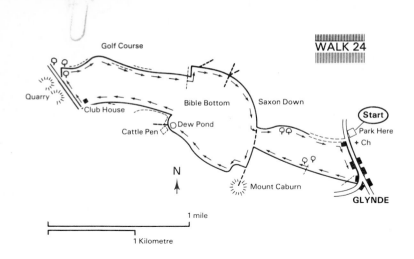

Quarry

Club House

Cattle Pen

Dew Pond

Bible Bottom

Saxon Down

Start

Park Here

+ Ch

N

Mount Caburn

GLYNDE

1 mile

1 Kilometre

hundred years and was at first undefended. In about 100 BC a bank and ditch were constructed, enclosing $3\frac{1}{2}$ acres, and several hundred people lived there. In addition to pottery, excavation has revealed weaving and agricultural tackle and an Iron Age razor. A massive outer rampart of chalk blocks with timber reinforcement was added later, possibly as a defence against the Romans, who eventually occupied the fort, having set fire to the timber gateway. They left behind scabbards and sword ornaments. All the finds can be seen in the Barbican House museum in Lewes.

From the summit, retrace your steps as far as a stile and metal gate about 150 yards beyond the outer ramparts of the hill-fort. Do not go over the stile but turn left just short of it on a rather ill-defined track which soon veers to the left and drops down to follow the bottom of a narrow valley. (This is not the precise line of the public footpath which is not easily usable on its correct line, but is the best route available.) Follow the bottom of the valley as it winds and gradually descends. After passing between a dewpond and a cattle pen, fork right with a fence on your left. In about 200 yards go left over a stile.

The dry valley to the right at this point is known as Bible Bottom because of the earthwork on the floor of the valley resembling an open book. Look out for some lynchets on the northern slope of the valley.

After crossing the stile, continue westwards along the side of the main valley with a fence still on your left. Keep along the fence line at first, but when it drops away to the left keep to the higher ground and climb gradually on the highest of a number of narrow paths cut into the hillside. This soon becomes a clear terraced track which you should follow, soon with another barbed wire fence to the left, up over the shoulder of the hill. Cross a stile by a metal gate and keep ahead on a rather uneven green strip across an open field. On reaching a golf

80

clubhouse, turn right and follow the access road downhill, with views over Lewes, which are seen best from the grass verge to the left of the road, along the rim of a chalk quarry.

A few yards after the road enters trees, fork right on a wide path which almost immediately doubles back to the right and climbs steeply up on to the Downs. Go over a stile and keep up the edge of grassy downland with a line of trees to the left. Where the trees bear away to the left, keep straight on. After passing another stile the footpath keeps straight on over the golf course and is undefined. To avoid flying golf balls it is probably best to edge fairly quickly to the right to pick up and follow the perimeter fence on the right of the golf course area. Cross a stile by a metal gate at the fourth tee, and follow a clear path along the side of the hill, parallel to and within sight of your outgoing route in the valley.

Follow this track round the rim of Bible Bottom. (From this height the 'open book' effect is a little more convincing.) After going through a gated double fence, turn sharply left and follow the double fence for 50 yards up to the crest of the ridge with a view ahead over the village of Ringmer and the Weald. At the top by a field gate, turn right and follow the ridge path, ignoring a track which forks to the left downhill. After going over a crossing track in a dip, go slightly right over a stile by a metal gate and continue on the wide grassy ridge path over Saxon Down. About 150 yards before reaching the point where you turned left on the ridge to climb to the top of Mount Caburn on the outgoing route, turn left on a clear track which drops and keeps to the left of a clump of trees. Where the path divides, keep right on the lower of two parallel tracks and follow it out to the road at Glynde.

Walk 25   Firle Beacon and the Old Coach Road

5½ miles (9 km)

OS sheets 198 and 199

This fairly easy walk would be worth doing if only for the pleasure of a
two-mile stretch along the old coach road at the foot of one of the most
splendid of downland escarpments, with continually changing views
of the noble profile of Firle Beacon. The walk ends along the ridgeway
with birds-eye views of West Firle village and the well wooded Firle
Park, and goes over the top of Firle Beacon with its fifty Bronze Age
barrows. The terraced bridleway by which the walk finally descends
the scarp slope is probably Roman in origin.

West Firle is an unusually attractive and unspoilt downland village
on the spring-line. The village spring remains to this day and was
probably used by villagers only a few generations ago. The route
crosses Firle Park within view of the handsome 18th century front of
Firle Place in its characteristically stately-home setting. The house is
on view to the public at certain times. The tower in the park was built
in the 19th century as a kind of game-keeper's lookout. The church is
mainly notable for a number of monuments to the Gage family who
have occupied Firle Place from the 15th century to the present day.

Alciston is an interesting village which can be visited with only a
slight detour from the described route. In medieval times Battle
Abbey had estates here. Since then the village has shrunk a great deal
but the fine and massive tithe barn remains as well as the ruins of a
medieval dovecote.

Park in the village of West Firle which is reached by turning right
(south) off the A27 Lewes–Eastbourne road about 5 miles east of
Lewes. There is reasonable roadside parking near the village post
office (OS map ref. 470072). Alternatively you can park at the top of
Bo-peep Bostal (as for Walk 26) and start the walk there.

Start the walk along a stony track which leaves the village street in
West Firle beside the post office and a telephone box. Notice the
spring which rises to the left of the path and is enclosed by a stone wall
with steps leading down to the water. The track leads you out into
Firle Park through a swing gate. Now follow a clear track across
parkland with Firle Place visible away to the right. Soon after crossing
the access drive to Firle Place, veer slightly to the right across open
parkland passing immediately to the left of a plantation and aiming
for a tower which can be seen ahead on a low hill (the tower is obvious

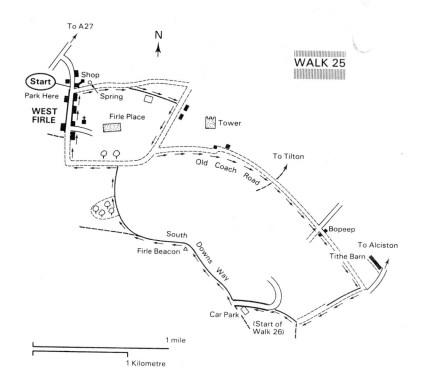

To A27

N

Start
Park Here
WEST
FIRLE

Shop
Spring
Firle Place

Tower

Old Coach Road

To Tilton

Bopeep

South
Firle Beacon △

Downs Way

To Alciston
Tithe Barn

Car Park

(Start of
Walk 26)

1 mile

1 Kilometre

in winter but tends to be obscured by tree foliage in summer). Join a wide track through a bridle gate and turn right along it.

Ignore a track to the left and go ahead with a flint wall on your right. At a T-junction turn left on to the old coach road which you now follow for over 2 miles along the foot of the Downs. In $1\frac{1}{2}$ miles go straight over the metalled access road to the Downs at Bo-peep.

Bo-peep is marked on the first edition of the one-inch Ordnance Survey map as Bo-peep gate. It has been surmised that the curious name comes from the turnpike keeper's way of peeping out of his small window, but, in fact, the 18th century turnpike road, which superseded the old coach road, followed the line taken by the present A27.

After another $\frac{1}{3}$ mile, soon after passing within sight of the Alciston tithe barn which can be seen, except in high summer, away through trees across a field to the left, you should turn right along the foot of a tree-lined bank. (To visit Alciston village, go straight on instead of turning right and almost immediately turn left. To rejoin the walk you must retrace your steps.)

After turning right along the foot of the bank, follow a path along the field edge at first. This leads gradually into a sunken enclosed track which climbs towards the Downs. This fine old track, locally reputed to have been an 18th century smugglers' route, was rescued from a state of total neglect and impassability a few years ago when it was cleared by volunteers belonging to the Sussex Rights of Way Group. It is now well used and is unlikely to become seriously obstructed again, but can be obscured by nettles in summer.

At the top of the sunken section of path, go over two stiles and turn right on a wide dirt track which brings you out on the metalled bostal road. Climb with this to the top of the Downs and the South Downs Way where you should turn right. (From this point at the top of the bostal Walk 26 starts.)

Follow the South Downs Way to the top of Firle Beacon where the triangulation point is at a height of over 700 feet. About 200 yards beyond the summit, go through a bridle gate and after another 300 yards go slightly right and gently downhill to follow a broken fence line along the top of the steepest part of the scarp slope. This will lead you to a clear terraced bridleway and you should follow this down to the foot of the hill. At the bottom, go through a bridle gate to the right of a wood and go along the left hand edge of a field with the wood on your left. Where the wood narrows after 250 yards go left through a gate opening and immediately turn right on a path within a line of trees. At a T-junction with a gate labelled 'Private' ahead, turn left on a wide track with a flint wall to the right and follow this back to the village of West Firle and the car.

Walk 26   Heighton Hill and Bishopstone

7½ miles (12 km)

OS sheets 198 and 199

To the east of the River Ouse the Downs are at their narrowest – less than half a day's walk from the northern escarpment to the sea. This walk starts on the crest of the Downs at a height of 620 feet and drops down almost to sea level at Bishopstone, crossing a stretch of empty, rolling downland. There are not many landmarks but the tracks are clear and good except for one short stretch which is often obliterated by ploughing. It is difficult to believe that just beyond this unspoilt downland there is a belt of modern building development which has crept up almost to the village of Bishopstone.

Bishopstone is a typical downland village with a good deal of flintwork and a large and beautiful church, one of the finest in Sussex. Bishopstone was part of the see of Chichester from the 8th century onwards and much of the church dates back to that time. There is a Saxon sundial over the porch which still bears the name of Eadric, presumably the mason or donor, and the fine early Norman tower is prominently visible from the surrounding hills with the village, a huddle of roofs and trees, clustered round it.

Park in the car parking area on the top of the Downs at Bo-peep Bostal (a link point with Walk 25). To get there turn right (south) off the A27 Lewes–Eastbourne road about 7 miles east of Lewes, soon after passing the Barley Mow at Selmeston. The turning is at OS map ref. 507065. Follow the narrow bostal road for about 1½ miles to the top of the Downs where there is a parking area at OS map ref. 494050.

From the point where the tarmac road turns left at the top of the Downs to go to the car park, keep straight on through two gates, passing to the right of a Dutch barn, and continue in a south-westerly direction with a fence on your left, for nearly ½ mile. On reaching a cattle pen on the left go through a gate and immediately turn right following another fence line. In 50 yards, do not follow the track round to the right but instead go through a rather awkward barbed wire gate and strike out diagonally downhill in a south-westerly direction across a large field, aiming for a gate a little to the left of a dark area of gorse which can be seen on the hill across the valley. (This field is often ploughed and planted without reinstatement of the path but it is probably better to follow the line of the right of way straight across the field rather than deviate round the edge because, unless a clear headland path has been left unploughed – and there was no sign of

85

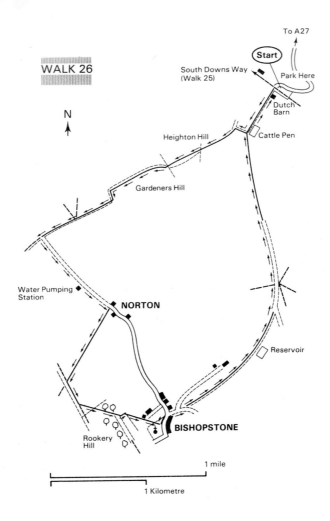

WALK 26

N

To A27

Start

South Downs Way
(Walk 25)

Park Here

Dutch
Barn

Cattle Pen

Heighton Hill

Gardeners Hill

Water Pumping
Station

NORTON

Reservoir

Rookery
Hill

BISHOPSTONE

1 mile

1 Kilometre

this when the path was checked – the amount of damage caused by walkers might well be greater using the headland route.)

Beyond the gate on the other side of this field, climb up over Heighton Hill, now on a good unploughed headland path with a fence line to the left. Go through another bridle gate on the summit and keep along the right hand edge of the next field on high ground with gorse bushes to the right. At the end of this field, follow the fence line

86

round to the left and, in 50 yards, go right over a stile to continue in a south-westerly direction, now with a fence and gorse on the left, over the shoulder of Gardeners Hill with the buildings of Newhaven in the distance ahead on the other side of the Ouse valley.

Drop down into a dip and climb again straight ahead, ignoring two tracks to the right. About two-thirds of the way up the other side, turn left on a broad track which drops back down into the valley which you then follow for nearly a mile. In just over $\frac{1}{2}$ mile, after passing a water pumping station on the right, the track becomes metalled.

Just before reaching the first house of the tiny hamlet of Norton, turn right through a green-painted metal field gate and follow a clear terraced track which curves to the left as it climbs to the top of the hill.

From the top there are views of Newhaven harbour ahead and to the left can be seen the cliffs of Seaford Head at the western end of the Seven Sisters (see Walk 28).

At the top, after passing under power lines, turn left along the ridge of Rookery Hill with a fence line on your right. In little more than 100 yards, begin to bear left downhill on a faintly defined path, aiming towards Bishopstone church which can be seen ahead in the valley. Go through a gate and follow an enclosed path which drops downhill through a belt of woodland. At the bottom of the hill, just as the path levels out, go left through two squeeze gates and along the edge of a field with a swampy area to the right and a flint wall on the left. After passing through a swing gate, go half right across an open field, aiming just to the left of the church. At the far corner of the field, go out through a gate and climb a rough slope ahead to a grassy area. Cross this and go out through the churchyard to the road in Bishopstone village.

At the road turn left and in about 50 yards, after passing a barn on the right and just before the road drops down, turn right on a wide track which climbs uphill. Ignore the first track to the left and in another 150 yards, where the main track turns right, go left along a grassy path and over a stile to follow a splendid terraced grassy track along the side of the hill, with a hedged bank to the right and the hill sloping quite steeply down to the left. After passing through a bridle gate continue on a clear path with a fence on your right, soon passing a reservoir on the right. Follow this clear headland track, first with a hedge to your right and subsequently parallel and to the left of a concrete track, eventually joining a bridleway coming in from the right and following it past another reservoir. At a junction with a number of ways, keep straight ahead on the main track and follow it along the side of Denton Hill, passing the curiously named site of three barrows known as Five Lords Burgh (burgh comes from the Old English *beorg* meaning mound or tumulus). Keep on this clear track for $1\frac{1}{2}$ miles before rejoining your outgoing route by the cattle pen. Retrace your steps to the car park.

Walk 27   Alfriston and the Long Man

6½ miles (10.5 km)

OS sheet 199

From Alfriston, this varied walk starts across arable land in the Cuckmere valley following well-used paths, then approaches the Downs at the foot of the giant hill figure known as the Long Man of Wilmington ('looking naked to the shires' in Kipling's famous phrase), and climbs right round him to get to the top of Windover Hill amongst the tumuli, both Bronze Age and Neolithic. It then strikes out across open downland towards the sea, and finally curves round the top of a dry valley and drops down to follow the Cuckmere river from Litlington back to Alfriston. There are some fine views, especially as you climb the track above the Long Man and look back at the long stretch of downland running towards Firle Beacon and the isolated Caburn range on the edge of the Ouse valley. The walk may be linked with Walk 30 (see text and sketch map) to give a combined circuit of 14½ miles.

    Alfriston is an attractive village which, despite great tourist pressures, retains a strong flavour of its past. There is a tiny market place, with a tree and the stump of a market cross, and some fine old buildings, including the Star, a beautiful half-timbered inn with an overhanging upper storey, built in the early 15th century, probably as a rest house for pilgrims and mendicant friars travelling to and from Chichester. It has been carefully preserved, the carvings on the front of the building picked out in bright colours as they probably would have been centuries ago. The lofty cruciform church is known as 'the cathedral of the Downs' and stands near the river on a mound, possibly of pagan religious origin. Nearby there is a pre-Reformation Clergy House, a humble place of timber and thatch, with a Sussex rammed chalk floor and a hall open to the sooty roof timbers. It was rescued from decay in 1896 and bought for £10 by the National Trust, the first building ever acquired by them, and is now open to the public.

    Alfriston was a centre of the smuggling industry in the 18th century, Cuckmere Haven nearby being a good landing place. As many as a dozen cutters would anchor off the beach and be met by two or three hundred smugglers on horseback. Everybody was involved. If you heard horses' feet at midnight you didn't look out of the window, as Kipling's poem makes clear – 'Watch the wall, my darling, while the Gentlemen go by'.

    Alfriston was also the centre of a sheep-rearing district in the days

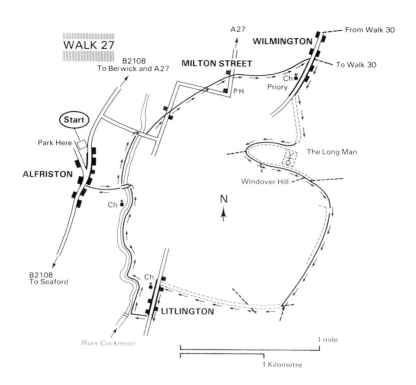

B2108
To Berwick and A27

MILTON STREET

A27

WILMINGTON

From Walk 30

To Walk 30

Ch
Priory

P.H.

Start

Park Here

ALFRISTON

Ch

The Long Man

Windover Hill

N

B2108
To Seaford

Ch

LITLINGTON

River Cuckmere

1 mile

1 Kilometre

when flocks of sheep were to be seen everywhere on the Downs. As recently as 1932 the old folk custom of laying a tuft of wool on a shepherd's breast at his funeral was observed here – a gentle hint to the Almighty that shepherds have to work on Sundays and cannot always manage to go to church.

Wilmington is little more than a single village street leading up to the church and the remains of an 11th century Benedictine priory, restored by the Sussex Archaeological Trust and open to the public. More interesting for most people, probably, is the Long Man cut in the hillside, 226 feet high, the largest chalk figure in England. Theories abound as to his origins, but nothing is known for certain.

Park at Alfriston. There is a large car park at OS map ref. 520033 in the middle of the village, which can get very overcrowded during the summer. There is limited alternative parking in Wilmington village street near the church and priory.

Leave the car park by the car exit and turn right on the main road. After passing the market cross and the Star inn on the right and the George inn on the left, turn left on a narrow path between houses,

89

which leads you to a bridge over the River Cuckmere. Do not cross the bridge, but turn left along the riverbank.

On reaching a road, turn right over the road bridge for 10 yards only before going left over a stile and diagonally half right across a field to another road where turn left. In 150 yards turn right through a bridle gate. Immediately inside the gate, turn left for 10 yards and then go right on a clear track. In another 30 yards go diagonally left off the main track on a narrower path which is usually well trodden out through the crop. Go straight over another road and then diagonally right across a field, aiming for a stile which is visible in the hedge. Keep straight on over the field beyond this stile to reach the road at Milton Street.

Turn left along the road for 60 yards before going right on a farm track. Follow this across a large field and out to the village street through Wilmington churchyard by way of a small iron gate to the rear of a stone seat and passing an ancient, much propped-up yew tree, claimed to be nearly 1000 years old and thus probably the oldest tree in Sussex. At the road turn right.

(To link with Walk 30 go straight across the road from the churchyard entrance and follow a clear track along the foothills of the Downs for about a mile to Folkington church, which is the starting point for Walk 30.)

To continue with Walk 27 follow the village street southwards past the priory. In 350 yards turn left on a track which leads up to the foot of the Long Man. About 150 yards before reaching the hill figure go through a bridle gate and fork right on a track which skirts the foot of an old quarry and then climbs round the shoulder of the hill. About 30 yards after going over a crossing track, go left through a bridle gate and climb on a path which soon runs parallel to the South Downs Way which at this point is a sunken chalk track. Where the South Downs Way veers to the right round the back of the hill, keep straight on with a fence to the left on a path which keeps to the left of the summit of Windover Hill and runs above the head of the Long Man.

After rejoining the South Downs Way on the other side of Windover Hill, follow it round the head of a combe and then bear right off the South Downs Way to keep along the left hand edge of the combe in a south-southwesterly direction with a fence and a line of gorse and scrub on your right. After passing through two bridle gates, the track winds through an area of scrub. On reaching a crossing track at a place called Winchester's Pond, turn right. In $\frac{1}{2}$ mile go straight over a wide oblique crossing track and drop downhill for another $\frac{1}{2}$ mile to exit through a farmyard on to the road at Litlington.

Turn left along the road passing Litlington church. In 300 yards, just beyond a shop on the right, turn right on a narrow tarmac path which leads you down to the River Cuckmere. Turn right and follow the river back to Alfriston. There is a public footpath on both river-banks.

Walk 28   Friston Forest and the Seven Sisters

7 miles (11 km)

OS sheet 199

This is a walk within an area designated by the Countryside Commission as 'Heritage Coast'. It crosses a series of landscapes which are now protected from development and largely open for public access. The Cuckmere valley from Exceat Farm to the sea is part of the Seven Sisters Country Park, Friston Forest belongs to the Forestry Commission, Crowlink and the rest of the Seven Sisters are in the care of the National Trust.

The last team of black oxen in Sussex was ploughing at Exceat Farm in 1922. It is now the Park Centre of the Country Park. The conversion has preserved the farm buildings and an old barn shelters an exhibition and book stall.

The sheltered downland village of Westdean is almost surrounded by Friston Forest. Adjoining the church, there is a 13th century parsonage, a solid flint house with narrow windows, originally without glass, which is thought to be one of the oldest inhabited houses in the country. It is possible that King Alfred had a manor house in the village. Charleston Manor, a mile to the north, is often open to the public and is well worth a visit.

Friston Forest is the only East Sussex equivalent of the many beech plantations on the West Sussex Downs. As you walk along the sheltered grassy rides, it is difficult to realize that the sea is so near. The forest is comparatively young, the trees still close together and fringed with nursery conifers.

The cliffs which make up the Seven Sisters must be nearly as famous as the white cliffs of Dover. They offer a most exhilarating walk which is rather strenuous because it involves crossing a succession of dry chalk valleys.

Walks 28 and 29 can be linked to give a combined length of $11\frac{1}{2}$ miles. Alternatively, if you would like to include in your walk all of the Seven Sisters (instead of only $4\frac{1}{2}$ of them), follow the described route of Walk 29 from the Crowlink car park as far as the cliff edge where you can turn right and follow the cliffs along to rejoin the main walk. This will add about a mile to the total.

Park at the Seven Sisters Country Park car park at Exceat. Exceat is on the A259 Seaford to Eastbourne road about 2 miles east of Seaford, and the car park is to the south of the road about $\frac{1}{4}$ mile east of the road bridge over the River Cuckmere (OS map ref. 519995).

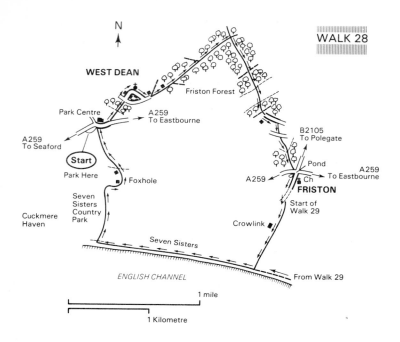

N

WEST DEAN

Friston Forest

Park Centre

A259
To Eastbourne

A259
To Seaford

B2105
To Polegate

Start

Pond

A259
To Eastbourne

Park Here

Foxhole

A259

Ch

FRISTON

Seven
Sisters
Country
Park

Start of
Walk 29

Cuckmere
Haven

Crowlink

Seven Sisters

ENGLISH CHANNEL

From Walk 29

1 mile

1 Kilometre

From the entrance to the car park, turn right along the A259 road for a
few yards, passing the Country Park Centre on the left. Immediately
beyond the centre, fork left on a roughly metalled track which leads
you into a field. Climb straight up the grassy hillside and over a stile in
a flint wall, passing a Forestry Commission notice and descending an
elaborate flight of steps to the village of Westdean. At the bottom,
keep straight on, ignoring turnings to right and left, and follow a
narrow road round to the right, passing the church on your left. About
100 yards beyond the church, turn left at a T-junction.

The road, metalled at first, soon becomes a forestry track. About 50
yards beyond a double gate, keep right on the lower main track. Soon
after passing a white-walled house on the left, fork left, still with the
main track which soon becomes a wide forest ride and climbs. Ignore
all side tracks and continue to ascend gently. Towards the top, views
open out to the left – northwards to Windover Hill on the escarpment
and westwards across the Cuckmere valley. After a full mile, turn
right at a wide crossing track. There are no obviously describable
features at this point, but the path to the left drops downhill and the
one to the right (your route) climbs at first and is a wide grassy ride.
All four tracks are, at the time of writing, waymarked with a blue
arrow, indicating bridleway status.

Follow the ride over a summit and downhill, ignoring side tracks.

92

At the bottom of a valley, go over a forestry track and climb again through more mature beech forest. After leaving the afforested area, keep straight ahead on a grassy path over open downland and drop down to re-enter the forest. Go over a metalled drive and in 100 yards go right through a gap in the scrub to the right of the path to join a parallel metalled driveway and turn left along it. About 50 yards short of a car passing place on the drive, look out for a narrow path on the right which takes you through a swing gate into a large field. Go half left across this field on a path which can usually be seen trodden out, and go through another swing gate in the flint wall ahead. Cross a driveway and go over a stile into another large field. Go diagonally uphill across this field and over a stile in the far corner into woodland. Now follow a clear track out to the road at Friston pond and church.

Follow the 'No through road' to Crowlink which starts between pond and church. In 300 yards go past the National Trust parking area on the right. (This is the starting point for Walk 29 and also for the extended Seven Sisters walk described above.)

Go ahead across a cattle grid and almost immediately fork left. Soon, fork left again and follow a track on high ground to the left of the Crowlink valley, traversing what must be one of the last remaining expanses of open permanent downland pasture in the entire South Downs. The buildings of Crowlink, nestling in the valley to your right, are now used as a holiday centre. On reaching the cliff edge you will find a sarsen stone commemorating the purchase of the Crowlink area in 1926 to provide public access and recreation.

Turn right along the cliff path and follow it over four of the Seven Sisters to the cliff above Cuckmere Haven. From here there are various routes back to the car park through the Seven Sisters Country Park. Here I will describe a good one.

Go right over a stile just before the cliff path drops into the Cuckmere valley. Follow the high ground along the side of the valley. Where the main path curves to the left and drops down, bear right and look out for a stile which takes you on to a path which descends into Foxhole Bottom, with its picturesque group of old farm buildings surrounded by sycamore trees. Keep round to the right of these buildings and then turn left and pass to the right of a modern barn. Go ahead through a bridle gate, and bear left over the shoulder of the hill, following a route waymarked with blue arrows back to the car park.

Walk 29   Friston and Belle Tout

4½ miles (7 km)

OS sheet 199

Another, shorter 'Heritage Coast' walk which can be linked with
Walk 28 to provide a total circuit of 11½ miles. It traverses part of the
National Trust Crowlink area, before dropping to Birling Gap and
climbing again to the old Belle Tout lighthouse, built in 1831. The
top, which housed the lantern, has now gone. The light was so often
obscured by sea-fog that the lighthouse at the foot of Beachy Head
was built to replace it in 1902. From the cliff top beyond Belle Tout
there are good views of the newer lighthouse.

The return walk passes through Eastdean, which, like Alfriston,
suffers from its popularity. The Tiger Inn, with its smuggling associa-
tions, and a group of flint and tile cottages surround the village green.
The nearby church has an unusually wide flint tower which may have
been built in this way to provide a refuge against raiders from the sea.
Birling Gap offered a landing place not far away and was used
centuries later by smugglers. Part of a row of coastguard cottages
survive from the 19th century at Birling Gap, the rest having fallen
into the sea, which is steadily eroding the whole length of chalk cliffs.

Friston lost its windmill years ago, but its characteristic downland
church remains exposed to the winds on the top of the hill, with the
old village pond nearby. Much of the church is Saxon and it has an
open timber roof dated about 1450. Little of the original village
remains, but a new village has spread fairly unobtrusively down the
hillside, merging with a similar development north of Eastdean.

Park at the National Trust car parking area at Crowlink. Turn
south off the A259 Seaford to Eastbourne road at Friston, about 4
miles east of Seaford. The turning is a 'No Through Road' which
starts between Friston pond and church almost opposite the B2105
turn-off. The car parking area is on the right in about 300 yards at OS
map ref. 550979.

To start the walk go back along the track by which you reached the
car park for 75 yards before going right through a field gate. Go
diagonally to the right across open pasture aiming for a swing gate
which can be seen in the fence ahead. Immediately beyond the gate
turn left and walk parallel to and a little way away from the fence line
on your left. Go through a bridle gate ahead and on through a narrow
belt of trees. Now take a well trodden path along the left hand edge of
pasture with woodland dropping away to the left, heading for a barn

WALK 29

with a red roof. After passing to the right of the barn, follow a path along the crest of Went Hill, eventually dropping down to the left of the ridge as you approach the cliff edge. Where the main track curves to the left, keep straight on through a field gate and subsequently a bridle gate. After passing some houses on the left, turn left and follow a wide track down to Birling Gap.

Take a narrow path which starts from the road at Birling Gap between a telephone box and a letter-box. Climb up on to the cliffs and follow the cliff edge path past a coastguard lookout and on for $\frac{1}{2}$ mile to the disused Belle Tout lighthouse. From the top there is a fine view back along the line of the Seven Sisters to Seaford Head. Keep to the left of the lighthouse buildings, and, as you continue along the cliff edge, the newer lighthouse comes into view at the foot of Beachy Head.

On reaching a road at a sharp bend, turn left and follow a grassy track which runs parallel and to the left of the road. In a little under $\frac{1}{4}$ mile, turn right and drop to the road on a grassy track. Go straight across the road and through a metal gate to follow a wide track, fenced on the left. In just under $\frac{1}{2}$ mile, where the main track curves to the right, go straight on, soon crossing a driveway through two bridle gates and continue on a clear track, eventually with a flint wall to your left. After going through a wooden field gate, turn left, keeping a wall and then a fence to your left. Pass to the right of the first of the buildings of Birling Farm and make your way out to a road through two metal swing gates.

Turn right along the road and follow it to the village of Eastdean; luckily there is a fairly wide grass verge. At the edge of the village fork left, signposted Eastdean village, and follow this road past the church on the right. On reaching the village green with a shop and the Tiger Inn beside it, turn sharply left along Went Way. In about 100 yards, turn right up some steps and climb on a narrow path with a flint wall to the right. This leads you out on to a sloping grassy hillside. Keep straight ahead uphill with a flint wall a little way away to the right. In 150 yards or so, turn right over the wall using some stone steps. Keep to the left of another wall which goes away at a right angle on the other side, and follow the right hand edge of pasture – you are now back on National Trust land. Where the fence on your right turns away to the right, keep straight ahead across open pasture and so back to the car park which you can see ahead.

The car park at the start and finish of this walk is the link point with Walk 28.

There is something very pleasing about the approach by road to the tiny village of Folkington (pronounced Fohwington), turning off the busy A27 along a quiet lane which leads to the foot of the Downs and comes to an abrupt end by the beautiful church among the trees.

From Folkington, the walk follows the old road along the foothills to Jevington, surely one of the most picturesque of all downland villages, half hidden by trees as you come down to it from the hill.

From Jevington the walk becomes very characteristic of the bare East Sussex downland, especially the gentle climb to the top of Babylon Down with its wide views over the Weald and the spread of Eastbourne towards Pevensey Levels.

This walk may be conveniently linked with Walk 27, giving a total distance of 14½ miles, including the one mile link with Wilmington. The east–west link is included with the route description of Walk 30 and a different west–east route is included with Walk 27.

Park at Folkington church. Turn left (south) off the A27 Eastbourne–Lewes road about a mile east of Polegate on to a narrow cul-de-sac road to Folkington. Park where the metalled road ends, just beyond Folkington church at OS map ref. 559038.

Start the walk by taking the left fork where the metalled road ends beyond Folkington church, dropping slightly downhill on a wide track which subsequently climbs and winds through the downland foothills for 1½ miles. Finally, at a T-junction with a wide chalky track, turn right and climb. In about 150 yards, fork left and follow the main track which soon becomes a sunken path between banks. In ¼ mile, when the path emerges on to an open green space, fork left and in 50 yards turn left at a T-junction. In another 10 yards or so, fork left downhill through woodland, continuing with your right to pass Jevington church and exit on to a road. Turn right for 15 yards before going left along Willingdon Lane. Where the lane ends keep straight ahead on a grassy track. In 150 yards fork left on the (slightly) higher of two tracks. After going through a field gate this becomes a well trodden path through scrub. Go on through a metal bridle gate and follow a wide track along the floor of Willingdon Bottom.

The left hand slope of this dry valley is marked on the map as a field system, rising towards the crest of Combe Hill, where there are traces of a Neolithic causewayed camp. Although the hillside is thick with

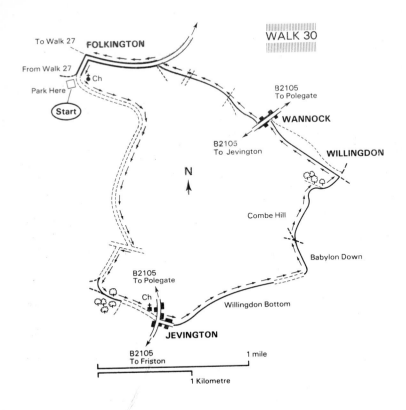

gorse, many of the lynchets can be seen, looking like great steps in the grass.

Where the valley divides into two, keep right through another metal bridle gate and climb on a clear fenced track out of the valley on to the top of Babylon Down. On reaching a car parking area turn left and follow the ridge of the downland with extensive views across Willingdon and Eastbourne to the sea. At a point in a dip where a number of paths converge, bear slightly right and take a path which drops down round the left hand edge of a combe, passing a wooden seat. Where the path forks half way down the hill, bear left round the shoulder. On reaching a belt of woodland, turn sharply right, dropping down along the edge of the wooded area. Fairly soon, go left through a swing gate and continue to descend with the wood on your left. In about 150 yards, turn left at a crossing track along a grassy headland path with a small cemetery to the right. Follow this stiled path, running parallel to the back gardens of houses, through two fields and on along an enclosed track beside allotments and out to the road at Wannock.

Turn left along the road for about 80 yards, and immediately after passing a house called Broadwater on the right, turn right between two small ponds. A few yards beyond a stile, bear left on a clear path, across an open field at first and then with a hedge to the left. Go over two stiles and across another field towards a line of trees on the skyline. On reaching the trees, go over a concrete track and another stile and follow a narrow path through a belt of woodland. Cross a stile into a field and bear left across it to a bridle gate in the left hand corner which takes you out into a road. Turn left on the road and follow it for a little over $\frac{1}{4}$ mile back to Folkington and the car.

To link with Walk 27, take a narrow track straight ahead into woods at the point where the road turns sharply left by the entrance to Folkington Manor. Follow this track through woodland and then on a rather overgrown section along the top edge of a field. After going through a broken bridle gate, turn right and keep round the right hand edge of the next field, continuing westwards along the right hand edge of the next two fields (parallel to the Downs) and out on a narrow enclosed path into Wilmington village street. Turn left and follow the street past the church and priory. You are now on Walk 27.